Northern
fleabane plant

owshoe
a horse

Eyewitness

ARCTIC &
ANTARCTIC

Written by
BARBARA TAYLOR

Photographed by
GEOFF BRIGHTLING

Carving of polar
bear from Canada

Model of Greenland canoe

Engraved ivory

Cribbage board made from walrus tusk

DK

**LONDON, NEW YORK,
MELBOURNE, MUNICH, AND DELHI**

Project editor Gillian Denton
Art editor Jane Tetzlaff
Managing editor Simon Adams
Managing art editor Julia Harris
Researcher Céline Carez
Editorial Assistance Djinn von Noorden, David Pickering
Production Catherine Semark
Picture research Clive Webster

REVISED EDITION

Revised by Richard Beatty & John Woodward

DK INDIA
Project editor Nidhi Sharma
Project art editor Rajnish Kashyap
Editor Pallavi Singh
Designer Mahipal Singh
Deputy managing editor Eman Chowdhary
Managing art editor Romi Chakraborty
DTP designer Tarun Sharma
Picture researcher Sumedha Chopra

DK UK
Senior editor Rob Houston
Senior art editor Philip Letsu
Production editor Tony Phipps
Publisher Andrew Macintyre

First published in Great Britain in 1995
This edition published in Great Britain in 2012
by Dorling Kindersley Limited,
80 Strand, London WC2R 0RL

10 9 8 7 6 5 4 3 2 1

001 – 183544 – Jan/12

Shaman's eagle from Siberia

Copyright © 1994; © 2000, © 2012 Dorling Kindersley Limited
A Penguin Company

Siberian shaman's apron

A CIP catalogue record for this book is
available from the British Library.

ISBN: 978-1-40539-462-8

Colour reproduction by Colourscan, Singapore
Printed and bound in China by
Toppan Printing Co. (Shenzhen) Ltd.

Discover more at

www.dk.com

Both the Arctic
and Antarctic support
some plant life

Husky dogs

Contents

Snowy owl

The ends of the Earth

THE TWO POLAR REGIONS at the very ends of the Earth are among the coldest, windiest, and most remote places on the planet. A huge, frozen ocean – the Arctic – surrounds the North Pole, while a vast area of frozen land – Antarctica – surrounds the South Pole (see maps on pp. 64–65). Both the Arctic and Antarctic have long, dark, freezing winters. During the short summer, the Sun shines all the time, and animals flock to polar areas to feed and nest. The Arctic and Antarctic are the last two wilderness areas on Earth. However, the Arctic has already been exploited for its mineral wealth, and both polar regions are increasingly threatened by climate change (see pp. 66–67).

TRAPPED BY THE ICE
In 1596, a Dutch explorer, William Barents, set off on his third attempt to find a route from Europe to China and India around the North Pole. When his ship was trapped by sea ice, he and his crew were forced to winter ashore, building a cabin from the wrecked ship. In spring, the men set off for Europe in the ship's boats. Barents himself died, but his men survived.

Arctic

Antarctic

The position of the Arctic and Antarctic

A WHITE WORLD
Ice dominates the landscapes and seascapes of the polar regions – as seen here in the Antarctic Peninsula. This peninsula is the most accessible part of the Antarctic continent to visiting tourist ships. Here, a summer scene is shown, with the sea ice broken up into small fragments. Once winter comes, the ocean becomes completely frozen over again.

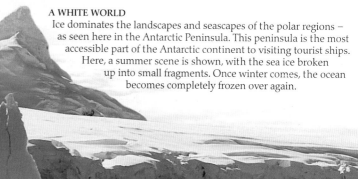

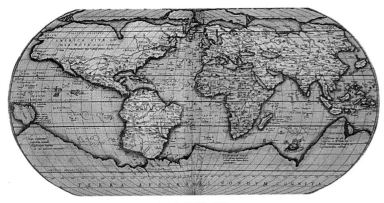

MYSTERY LAND

In the 4th century BCE, the Greek philosopher Aristotle suggested the existence of a southern landmass, known in Latin as *Terra Australis Incognita* – the unknown southern continent. Map-makers included a huge southern continent on their maps until 1773, but it was not until Captain James Cook's exploration in the mid-18th century that anyone knew what was really there.

NORTHERN LIGHTS

Auroras are wispy curtains of light that appear in the sky above the poles. They can sometimes take the form of brilliantly coloured shooting rays. Auroras are caused by charged particles from the Sun striking gases in the Earth's atmosphere above the poles. This makes the gases give off light.

MIDNIGHT SUN

In regions near the North and South poles, the Sun never sets for several months during the summer. This happens because of the tilt of the Earth towards the Sun. While one pole has constant daylight the other is shrouded in winter darkness because the Sun never rises.

Land ice is built up from centuries of falling snow and is much thicker than sea ice. It flows slowly downhill and may extend over the sea as an ice shelf

Broken fragment of ice shelf – a vast iceberg

Sea ice is usually less than 5 m (16 ft) thick. This small fragment here is probably less than 1 m (3 ft) thick. Sea ice may be continuous, as it is over much of the Arctic Ocean, or in fragments

Small, melted fragment of iceberg

The Arctic and tundra

At the centre of the Arctic region is a vast area of permanently frozen ice floating on the Arctic Ocean. The Arctic region also includes the largest island in the world, Greenland, the island of Spitsbergen, and the northern edges of North America, Asia, and Europe. South of the Arctic Ocean is the tundra, which means "treeless plain" in Russian. The landscape is low and flat, with many lichens, mosses, grasses, and sprawling, low bushes. Trees cannot grow in the true Arctic because they are unable to stand up to the intense cold and fierce winter winds. The main sea connection of the Arctic Ocean is with the Atlantic, whose warmer waters push back the point at which permanent ice exists.

MAPPING THE COAST
In 1819–22, Sir John Franklin, who later lost his life searching for the elusive Northwest Passage (p. 52), made a hazardous land expedition charting the coast of Canada. At one point he took a canoe which was particularly hazardous as the ice was breaking up. Wooden ships and boats of the 19th century could easily be crushed or trapped by ice.

Marshy pools form because permafrost prevents water from draining away

The 'tree line' where forest gives way to tundra, is often taken to be the southern boundary of the true Arctic

Frozen layer, called permafrost, lies a little way below the surface

BEAR JOURNEYS
Polar bears live only in the Arctic. They make long journeys across the Arctic sea ice, hunting for seals. The bears are expert divers and swimmers and often hitch rides on ice floes. One polar bear was found swimming 320 km (200 miles) from land. Polar bears can also dive more than 15 m (50 ft) from the top of icebergs into the water.

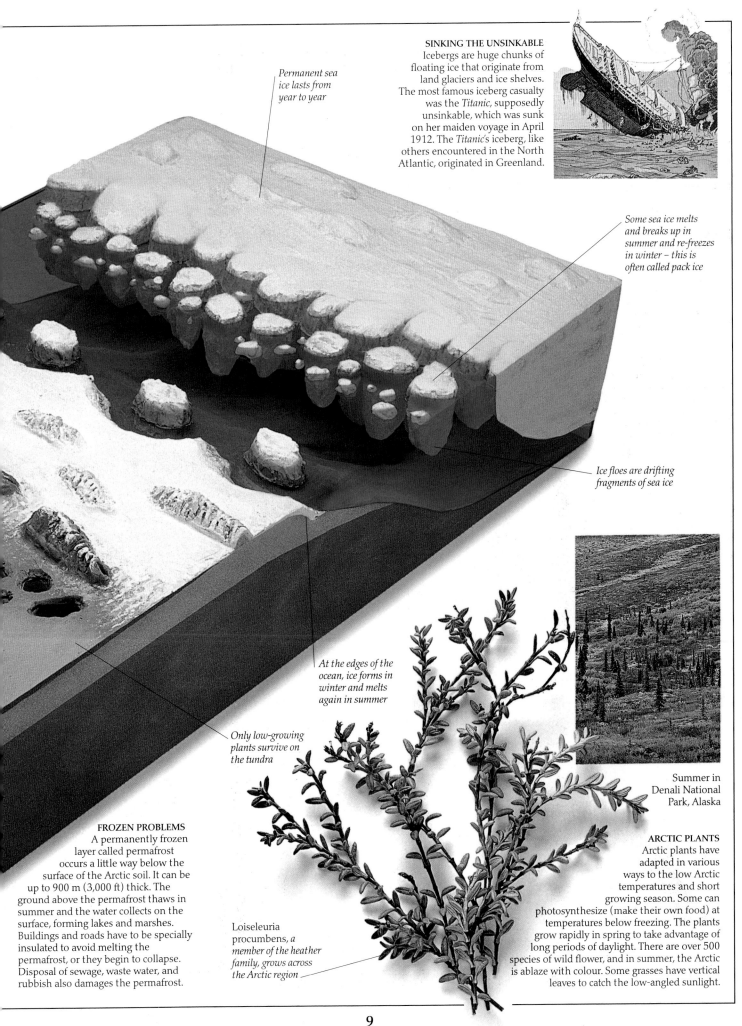

Permanent sea
ice lasts from
year to year

SINKING THE UNSINKABLE
Icebergs are huge chunks of
floating ice that originate from
land glaciers and ice shelves.
The most famous iceberg casualty
was the *Titanic*, supposedly
unsinkable, which was sunk
on her maiden voyage in April
1912. The *Titanic's* iceberg, like
others encountered in the North
Atlantic, originated in Greenland.

Some sea ice melts
and breaks up in
summer and re-freezes
in winter – this is
often called pack ice

Ice floes are drifting
fragments of sea ice

At the edges of the
ocean, ice forms in
winter and melts
again in summer

Only low-growing
plants survive on
the tundra

Summer in
Denali National
Park, Alaska

FROZEN PROBLEMS
A permanently frozen
layer called permafrost
occurs a little way below the
surface of the Arctic soil. It can be
up to 900 m (3,000 ft) thick. The
ground above the permafrost thaws in
summer and the water collects on the
surface, forming lakes and marshes.
Buildings and roads have to be specially
insulated to avoid melting the
permafrost, or they begin to collapse.
Disposal of sewage, waste water, and
rubbish also damages the permafrost.

*Loiseleuria
procumbens, a
member of the heather
family, grows across
the Arctic region*

ARCTIC PLANTS
Arctic plants have
adapted in various
ways to the low Arctic
temperatures and short
growing season. Some can
photosynthesize (make their own food) at
temperatures below freezing. The plants
grow rapidly in spring to take advantage of
long periods of daylight. There are over 500
species of wild flower, and in summer, the Arctic
is ablaze with colour. Some grasses have vertical
leaves to catch the low-angled sunlight.

The Antarctic

THE CONTINENT OF ANTARCTICA is twice the size of Australia, and one and a half times the size of the US. It is also three times higher than any other continent – almost all of it is covered by an ice sheet that is, on average, 2,500 m (8,000 ft) thick. This height is a major reason for the extreme cold in Antarctica, where the average winter temperature is –60°C (–76°F). Antarctica's severe climate, and its isolation from other continents, has greatly reduced the variety of its wildlife – the largest animal that lives on land all year round is a tiny insect. During the summer, however, many animals including penguins, whales, and seals, visit the continent to take advantage of the plentiful food supply and safe breeding sites. Plants are very sparse and consist mostly of lichens, mosses, and liverworts.

HARDY SURVIVOR
Among the few types of living thing able to grow on land in Antarctica are lichens. A lichen is a double organism, in which a fungus teams up with a simple plant (alga). Lichens are slow growing and can resist extreme conditions well.

WARMER CLIMATE
Antarctica was not always cold. Fossil ferns (above) provide evidence of a warmer, subtropical climate about 70 million years ago, even in polar regions. But the plants would still have experienced several months of darkness each year.

SOUTH POLE PENGUINS
Penguins live only in the southern hemisphere. In the Arctic, auks have a similar lifestyle to penguins. They also look like penguins, but auks can fly, and penguins cannot.

Only 10 per cent of an iceberg is visible above water level

ICEBERGS
Icebergs form when snow falls on the Antarctic plateau and turns into ice. The ice is compacted, and flows down towards the coastal ice shelves where it is broken up by ocean tides, currents, and waves. This produces icebergs. Some icebergs are so large – up to 240 km (150 miles) long and 110 km (70 miles) wide – that they can be tracked by satellites for several years before they melt.

COILED CLUES
Swimming shellfish with coiled shells, called ammonites, were common in subtropical seas of prehistoric times. The last ammonites died out about 65 million years ago, but fossil ammonites found on Antarctica show that Antarctic seas were warmer millions of years ago.

WEIGHT OF ICE
About 98 per cent of Antarctica is covered by an immense ice sheet, which in some places is over 4 km (2.5 miles) thick. Most of the mountains, and all the lower ground is buried under ice. Only a few jagged peaks, called nunataks, stick out. The enormous weight of the ice pushes most of the rocky surface of Antarctica below sea level. The ice in the lowest layers of the ice sheet is thought to be at least 200,000 years old.

DRY VALLEYS
Hidden among the Transantarctic Mountains are vast dry valleys, which are not covered by snow or ice all year round. The valleys originally dried out because the mountains held back the ice cap. Winds rushing down the valleys suck away any moisture, forming large areas of bare rock in the middle of the continent.

CLEARING THE ICE
Special ships called icebreakers are used to clear routes through frozen polar seas. Before icebreakers, many early polar explorers saw their fragile wooden ships crushed by the power of the ice. Icebreakers have a specially shaped bow and a reinforced hull. They push the bow on top of the ice until the weight of the ship breaks through it.

As icebergs melt, they often form fascinating shapes

The erosive forces of ocean and winds combine to carve the ice

Life in Antarctic waters

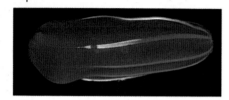

COMMON CREATURES
Antarctic squid (top) have no shell, which may be useful in icy waters where shells grow very slowly. They seize prey in their two long tentacles. Some types of comb jelly (bottom) are also common predators in Antarctic waters.

IN CONTRAST TO THE SMALL VARIETY of animals on land, there is an incredible wealth of life in the sea around Antarctica. In shallow waters, ice scrapes against the sea bed preventing any life, but in deeper waters below the crust of ice, there is a greater variety of life in the Antarctic Ocean than in the Arctic Ocean. Corals and anemones are anchored to the seabed with some 300 varieties of sponges. Many sea creatures feed on each other or on dead plankton. The cold affects the life cycles of many inhabitants. Because food is scarce most of the year, animals function more slowly. They produce fewer, larger eggs and look after them with care. Many animals live longer than their counterparts in warmer waters. Some sponges live for several centuries.

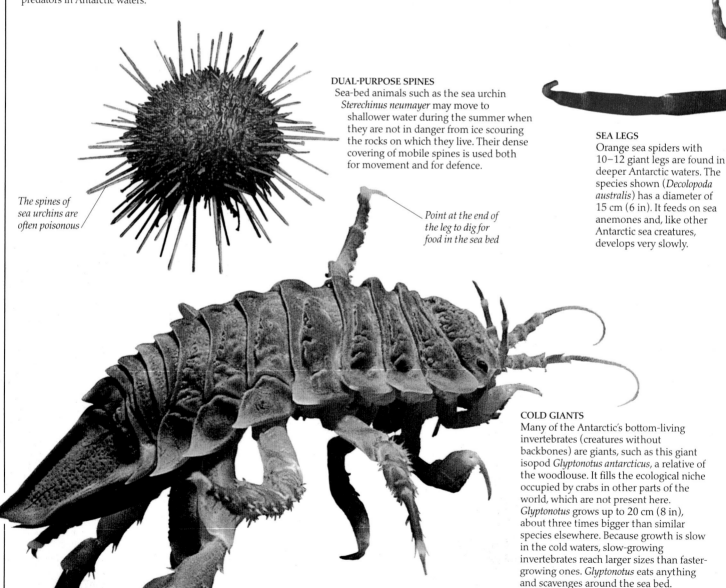

DUAL-PURPOSE SPINES
Sea-bed animals such as the sea urchin *Sterechinus neumayer* may move to shallower water during the summer when they are not in danger from ice scouring the rocks on which they live. Their dense covering of mobile spines is used both for movement and for defence.

The spines of sea urchins are often poisonous

Point at the end of the leg to dig for food in the sea bed

SEA LEGS
Orange sea spiders with 10–12 giant legs are found in deeper Antarctic waters. The species shown (*Decolopoda australis*) has a diameter of 15 cm (6 in). It feeds on sea anemones and, like other Antarctic sea creatures, develops very slowly.

COLD GIANTS
Many of the Antarctic's bottom-living invertebrates (creatures without backbones) are giants, such as this giant isopod *Glyptonotus antarcticus*, a relative of the woodlouse. It fills the ecological niche occupied by crabs in other parts of the world, which are not present here. *Glyptonotus* grows up to 20 cm (8 in), about three times bigger than similar species elsewhere. Because growth is slow in the cold waters, slow-growing invertebrates reach larger sizes than faster-growing ones. *Glyptonotus* eats anything and scavenges around the sea bed.

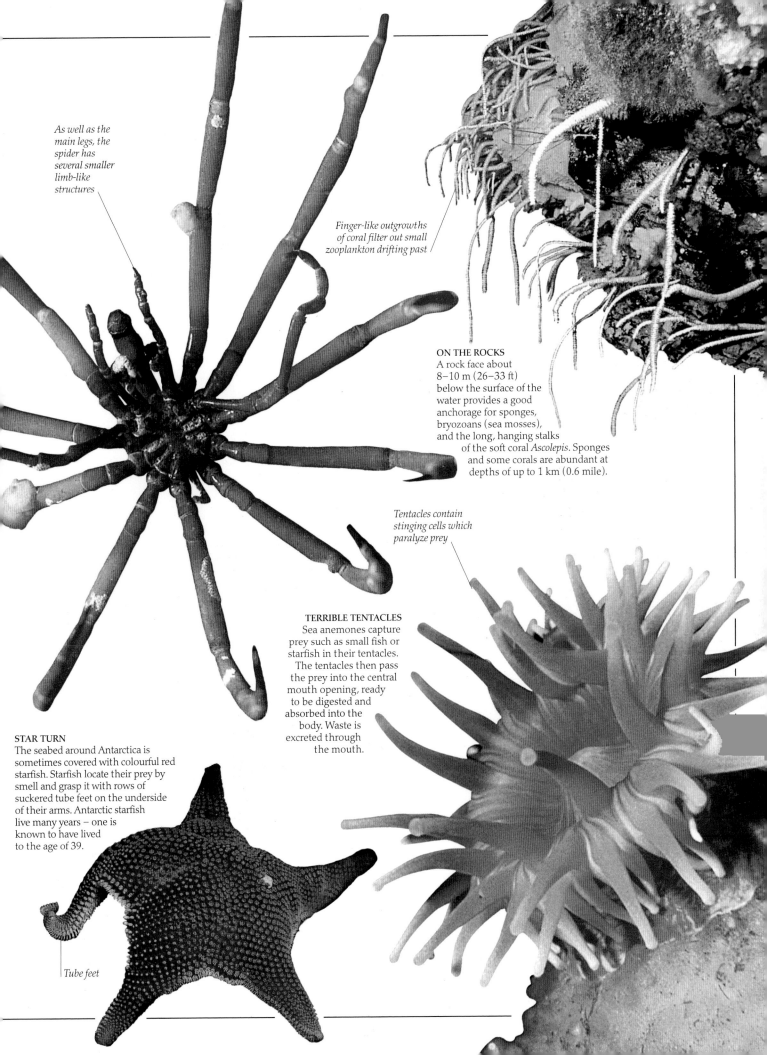

As well as the main legs, the spider has several smaller limb-like structures

Finger-like outgrowths of coral filter out small zooplankton drifting past

ON THE ROCKS
A rock face about
8–10 m (26–33 ft)
below the surface of the
water provides a good
anchorage for sponges,
bryozoans (sea mosses),
and the long, hanging stalks
of the soft coral *Ascolepis*. Sponges
and some corals are abundant at
depths of up to 1 km (0.6 mile).

Tentacles contain stinging cells which paralyze prey

TERRIBLE TENTACLES
Sea anemones capture
prey such as small fish or
starfish in their tentacles.
The tentacles then pass
the prey into the central
mouth opening, ready
to be digested and
absorbed into the
body. Waste is
excreted through
the mouth.

STAR TURN
The seabed around Antarctica is
sometimes covered with colourful red
starfish. Starfish locate their prey by
smell and grasp it with rows of
suckered tube feet on the underside
of their arms. Antarctic starfish
live many years – one is
known to have lived
to the age of 39.

Tube feet

Migrants and residents

THE NUMBER AND VARIETY of animals living near the poles change dramatically with the seasons. Thousands of birds and mammals only visit the Arctic or Antarctic during the brief, light summer months, when it is relatively warm and there is plenty of food available, day and night. Apart from the food supply, the other advantages for summer migrants are safe places to rear their young, with few predators, and a lack of competition for food and nesting places. Often, the same traditional migration routes are used each year, but the animals also navigate using the positions of the Sun, Moon, and stars, the Earth's magnetic field, and familiar landmarks. Journeys are often very dangerous, and many animals are killed by bad weather, lack of food, and predators before reaching their destination.

Dense down feathers help to keep the geese warm

The birds save energy by flying in a V-formation in the slipstream of the one in front

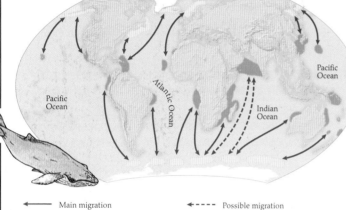

Pacific Ocean

Atlantic Ocean

Indian Ocean

Pacific Ocean

⟵ Main migration

◀---- Possible migration

▓ Major feeding areas (summer)

▓ Major feeding areas (winter)

FOOD IN THE FREEZER
Humpback whales in both the Northern and the Southern hemispheres travel to cold polar waters in summer to take advantage of the rich food supply of plankton and fish. In winter, when the sea freezes over, they migrate back to warmer tropical waters again to breed. They eat little during their tropical stopover, relying on their immense supply of body fat, built up during the summer.

Thick skull and solid, horny band protect the brain when males clash horns

Musk ox
Ovibos moschatus

Efficient wings allow the tern to cover up to 40,000 km (25,000 miles) on each round trip

Very long outer fur retains body warmth and keeps animal dry

CHAMPION TRAVELLER
The graceful Arctic tern may see more daylight each year than any other creature. It breeds in large colonies during the Arctic summer. It then flies all the way to the Antarctic to take advantage of the almost constant daylight and rich food supply of the Antarctic summer.

Arctic tern
Sterna paradisaea

MIGHTY MUSK OX
Tough, hardy musk oxen roam over the harsh tundra in herds made up of females and young, led by one or more strong bulls. In summer, herds number about ten animals, but in winter, musk oxen move south in herds of 50 or more, wherever they can find food under the snow. Their name comes from the smell given off by the males during the breeding season.

The male's antlers are larger and thicker than those of the females

Caribou
Rangifer tarandus

Caribou can move over soft ground or snow without sinking deeply

FLIGHT OF THE SNOW GEESE
Many thousands of pairs of snow geese nest in the Arctic tundra in the summer. They migrate all the way from the Gulf of Mexico, a journey of about 3,200 km (2,000 miles). On their journey, they fly in flocks of tens of thousands of birds. The shorter days at the end of summer tell the snow geese it is time to fly south once more.

SUMMER HOLIDAYS
Caribou herds are always on the move, wandering between their winter and summer feeding grounds and snatching bites of food wherever they can find it. In spring, immense herds trek northwards to feed on lichens and other low-growing tundra plants. They use well-marked trails that are often centuries old. As winter closes in, the caribou move south once more to the shelter of the forests.

Feet are tucked back during flight to make a more streamlined shape

Snow goose
Anser caerulescens

Dense woolly underfur and thick layers of fat under the skin keep the musk ox warm

Curved horns used to defend animals against predators such as wolves

Short, very strong legs support the massive body

Edges of hoofs are sharp enough to dig through thick snow and ice to reach mosses, lichens, and roots underneath

15

Adaptable animals

To SURVIVE THE CONTRASTING SEASONS, animals have to act. As winter approaches, some mammals' fur coats grow thick. Winter fur is often white, which helps to camouflage the animal against snow. A thick layer of fat in their skin traps extra warmth and acts as a food store in lean times. Birds also have layers of fat and dense, fluffy feathers, which keep out the cold. For many birds and mammals, the severe winter weather is just too much to cope with. They migrate south to warmer places, returning again in spring. Insects lay their eggs when the soil is warm, and the larvae can withstand the freezing temperatures of winter. As summer arrives, birds and mammals moult their thick coats. Animals that turn white in winter, often turn brown for summer camouflage.

FINE FURS
People in cold countries have always worn fur hats to keep warm through the winter. They usually obtained the warm fur by snaring their original owners in traps.

Arctic fox
Alopex lagopus

DRESSED FOR SUMMER
In summer, the Arctic fox grows a thinner coat of brownish-grey fur over most of its body. These colours match the brownish-grey rocks of the tundra landscape, making the fox hard to see, so that it can creep up on its prey, such as lemmings, without being spotted. The fox stores food under rocks during the summer and comes back to eat it in the winter months when food is hard to find. Arctic foxes have a varied diet, eating anything from berries, shells, and dead animals to rubbish, birds, and eggs.

The chest and belly are usually a pale greyish white

Short legs (and tail) lose less heat than long ones, as there is less surface area exposed to the air

Thick, bushy tail can be curled around the body for warmth during blizzards or when resting or sleeping

Antarctic ice fish
Chaenocephalus aceratus

ANTI-FREEZE IN ITS VEINS
Many Antarctic fish have anti-freeze molecules in their bodies that enable them to live in a "supercooled" state; their body fluids remain liquid at temperatures below the point at which ice forms. Antarctic ice fish (such as the fish on the left) have almost translucent (see-through) blood.

Hair under paws stops fox sinking in snow; the fox's Latin name is Alopex lagopus. Lagopus means "hairy foot".

Sharp claws to dig through the snow to find food

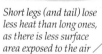

A BIRD FOR ALL SEASONS
Ptarmigans change their plumage twice a year, so that they are well camouflaged at all times. They also increase their feather density in winter. When resting overnight, they sometimes burrow in snow to reduce heat loss.

Rock ptarmigan
Lagopus mutus

Dense fur coat with long hairs traps body warmth

Ears are furry inside and out for extra warmth

FINE TO BE FAT
Whales and seals are kept warm by a layer of thick fat called blubber. This fat walrus is in no danger of getting cold. Walruses can weigh up to 1,600 kg (1.6 tons), with tusks 1 m (3 ft) long.

Small, round ears and a short muzzle cut down on heat loss; foxes from warmer places have larger ears and a longer muzzle

Sharp, pointed teeth to grab animals such as lemmings

DOUBLE-GLAZED FUR
The Arctic fox's white winter fur is made up of hairs which are hollow inside, full of air. The air in the hairs traps body warmth from the fox in much the same way as a double-glazed window traps warmth from houses. Air is a good insulator and does not let heat pass through it easily. The Arctic fox can tolerate temperatures of –40°C (–40°F), or even lower, quite comfortably.

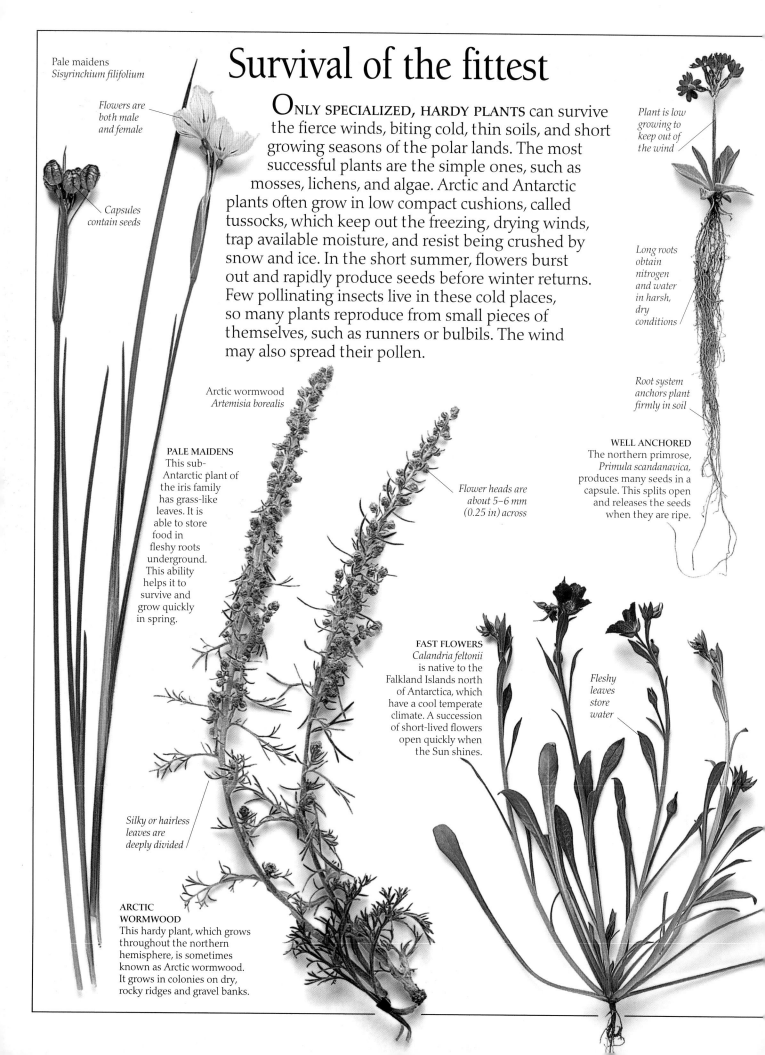

Pale maidens
Sisyrinchium filifolium

Flowers are both male and female

Capsules contain seeds

Survival of the fittest

ONLY SPECIALIZED, HARDY PLANTS can survive the fierce winds, biting cold, thin soils, and short growing seasons of the polar lands. The most successful plants are the simple ones, such as mosses, lichens, and algae. Arctic and Antarctic plants often grow in low compact cushions, called tussocks, which keep out the freezing, drying winds, trap available moisture, and resist being crushed by snow and ice. In the short summer, flowers burst out and rapidly produce seeds before winter returns. Few pollinating insects live in these cold places, so many plants reproduce from small pieces of themselves, such as runners or bulbils. The wind may also spread their pollen.

Plant is low growing to keep out of the wind

Long roots obtain nitrogen and water in harsh, dry conditions

Root system anchors plant firmly in soil

Arctic wormwood
Artemisia borealis

Flower heads are about 5–6 mm (0.25 in) across

PALE MAIDENS
This sub-Antarctic plant of the iris family has grass-like leaves. It is able to store food in fleshy roots underground. This ability helps it to survive and grow quickly in spring.

WELL ANCHORED
The northern primrose, *Primula scandanavica*, produces many seeds in a capsule. This splits open and releases the seeds when they are ripe.

FAST FLOWERS
Calandria feltonii is native to the Falkland Islands north of Antarctica, which have a cool temperate climate. A succession of short-lived flowers open quickly when the Sun shines.

Fleshy leaves store water

Silky or hairless leaves are deeply divided

ARCTIC WORMWOOD
This hardy plant, which grows throughout the northern hemisphere, is sometimes known as Arctic wormwood. It grows in colonies on dry, rocky ridges and gravel banks.

Woolly bear caterpillar
Arctia caja

PLANT EATER
There are several types of butterfly and moth living in Arctic regions.

Branched flower head is called a panicle

Northern fleabane
Erigeron borealis

Side branches have spikelets on stalks

Daisy-like flowers made up of small flowers called florets

Slipperwort
Calceolaria fothergillii

Large, lower petals look like a slipper

INSECT REPELLANT
Low cushions of northern fleabane flower in the Arctic summer when the tundra lands become waterlogged with melted ice and snow. The plant is highly unattractive to fleas and midges, hence its name, and is used by humans as an insect repellant.

Flower sticks out from leaves so insects can spot the flower easily

GROWTH OF GRASS
The most successful plants in the cold polar regions are the low-lying mosses and lichens. However, several grasses, such as *Deschampsia cespitosa*, thrive in the Arctic. On the Antarctic mainland, only one grass survives: *Deschampsia flexuosa*, or Antarctic wavy-hair grass.

Hairy leaves trap warmth and moisture

SLIPPERWORT
This rare and beautiful slipper-flower grows along the coasts of the Falkland Islands. The colour of the large, slipper-like lower petal attracts insects. Pollen sticks to them while feeding on the plant's nectar and is carried to another slipperwort, helping it to reproduce.

TREELESS TUNDRA
The tundra is a broad zone of low-growing vegetation lying immediately south of the Arctic Ocean across northern Eurasia and North America, where the harsh climate, severe winds, and shallow, frozen soils prevent trees from growing. The small plants of the tundra grow slowly and are nearly all perennial (live longer than a year).

Birds of the Arctic

Few birds can survive the hostile Arctic climate all year round, but residents include the ptarmigan, raven, ivory gull, and little auk. The plumage of Arctic residents is more dense than that of migratory species, especially in the winter, and their feet, protected by feathers, do not freeze to the ice. Most Arctic birds, such as waders, ducks, geese, swans, and gulls, are migratory. Some migrants, particularly waders, travel long journeys in winter, as far as South America, South Africa, and Australasia. In summer, Arctic birds take advantage of the rich insect and small mammal life on the tundra, nesting and rapidly rearing young before the winter sets in. Many different types of bird can feed and nest in close proximity because they share out the available food; for instance, geese eat plants, seabirds eat fish, and waders eat invertebrates.

LIKE A BIRD
In 1926, the airship *Norge* carried Norwegian Roald Amundsen and Italian Umberto Nobile over the North Pole.

HAPPY FAMILIES
The little auk (*Alle alle*) is not much bigger than a thrush, but there are a lot of them! Over 100 million little auks, or dovekies, breed along Arctic coasts each summer. In winter, they move south but usually stay near the Arctic Circle. Little auks have a thick layer of fat under the skin to keep warm. They feed on small invertebrates and fish, storing food in a throat pouch.

Straight, powerful beak for stabbing prey

Long neck to probe in water beds

ON DISPLAY
Cranes mate for life and perform spectacular courtship dances, head bobbing, bowing, skipping and sometimes leaping as high as 6 m (20 ft) in the air.

Streamlined, torpedo-shaped body allows fast underwater swimming

RED HEADS
Sandhill cranes (*Grus canadensis*) breed mostly in the remote Arctic, laying their eggs in mounds of grass or other plants in an undisturbed marsh. Young birds stay with their parents for nearly a year. The sandhill crane's plumage often appears rusty because of reddish iron oxide stains from the water of tundra ponds. The birds probe with their bills in the mud for worms, water creatures, and frogs, then transfer the stain to their feathers when preening.

A BIRD IN THE NET
Arctic birds were an invaluable source of food for Inuit people. They often caught the birds in nets on long poles.

Moving the two sticks back and forth causes the birds to bob down for their food

TOY TIME
Carving is an ancient Inuit art which often shows Arctic birds and mammals. The villages of Holman Island and Cape Dorset in Canada have become well known for their style of art. To make this bird-feeding toy work, the two sticks are moved back and forth.

Powerful, slender, dagger-shaped beak snaps up fish and crustaceans

FEATHER BEDS
Eider ducks (*Somateria mollissima*) in the Arctic are migratory, whereas in warmer places they stay near their breeding grounds all year. Eider ducks feed mainly on shellfish which they swallow whole. Muscles in the bird's stomach crush the shellfish. Eider ducks have particularly soft and dense down feathers for warmth. Female eiders pluck some of their breast feathers to line their nests. People use these feathers to fill quilts.

LOONY BIRDS
Divers, such as this black-throated species, are called loons in North America. Loons are adapted to swimming underwater after their prey and are clumsy on land because their legs are set so far back on the body. The name loon may come from the Icelandic word *lomr*, meaning lame or clumsy. The black-throated diver or Arctic loon breeds on tundra lakes and migrates mainly to the Pacific coast in winter.

Handsome breeding plumage; winter plumage is dull and greyish

WATER LOVERS
Divers spend most of their lives on the water and only come on land to nest. Puffins (foreground) are also excellent swimmers and divers, hunting for small shoaling fish such as sand eels. They are ungainly on land but are able to jump from rock to rock.

Birds of the Antarctic

THE MOST COMMON ANTARCTIC BIRDS are seabirds such as penguins, albatrosses, and petrels, which come ashore in summer to breed in remote, predator-free locations. They take advantage of the seas around Antarctica, which are packed with food for hungry chicks. Only 13 species of flying bird make use of ice-free land for nesting on the Antarctic mainland. The rest squash into colonies on equally cramped sub-Antarctic islands. Antarctic birds rely on their dense feathers and frostbite-resistant feet to keep warm, while fat reserves in the skin act as both food reserves and insulation. Most Antarctic birds leave during the cold winter months. But some, including emperor penguins, king penguins, and wandering albatrosses, stay behind to complete their long breeding cycle. Others, such as sheathbills, only just manage to survive in the freezing winter conditions.

ANTARCTIC SCAVENGERS
Giant petrels are nicknamed "stinkers" because of their unpleasant smell. They use their powerful, hooked beaks for feeding and scavenging, as well as killing other birds. Petrels will eat almost anything, including dead seals and whales. A petrel is about the size of a vulture, with a wingspan of nearly 2 m (6.5 ft).

Wings are held up like a Viking helmet, making the bird appear large and fierce

Ear-splitting shriek warns enemies to keep away

Powerful hooked beak stabs and kills prey

Antarctic skua
Catharacta maccormicki

Wings are spread to display white patches

PIRATES OF THE SKIES
Peculiar, dog-like barking calls signal the arrival of a pair of skuas. Skuas live up to their reputation as "pirates of the skies" by chasing other birds, forcing them to regurgitate their food. These large, aggressive birds are also notorious for stealing the eggs and young of other birds. Two skuas may even cooperate while hunting, using clever tricks to snatch a meal more easily.

Brown skua
Catharacta lonnbergi

NOT FUSSY
Sheathbills are the only land birds able to scrape a living in Antarctica. Their success is due to their varied diet, which includes penguin and seal faeces, penguin eggs, chicks, dead fish, krill, and limpets. Sheathbills also steal food intended for penguin chicks.

Horny sheath protects nostrils

Orange growths at base of beak become brighter during breeding season

Jagged, hooked bill helps to grip slippery fish

Blue-eyed shag
Phalacrocorax atriceps

Wings are spread out to dry off after a swim

Feathers soak up water and allow the shag to dive more easily

Tern

Albatross

Shearwater

Cormorant

Penguin

DIFFERENT STROKES
The pursuit of a fishy meal involves a different technique for every type of bird. Cormorants use their strong feet to paddle deep underwater after prey, while penguins dive deep and propel themselves through the sea using their wings. A tern picks fish by plunging down just under the surface of the water, while albatrosses float on the surface keeping a sharp eye out for any likely food. Shearwaters spot their prey from the air and then plunge in pursuit.

SEAWEED NEST
Blue-eyed shags nest in smelly, noisy colonies close to the sea, building untidy nests of seaweed, lichens, mosses, and feathers glued together with guano (bird excrement). Blue-eyed shags breed on the Antarctic Peninsula and on a number of Antarctic and sub-Antarctic islands. Some use their nesting sites all year round, roosting there throughout the winter. This allows them to stay near their fishing grounds in the open water.

Snowy owl
Bubo scandiacus

Lords of the skies

The huge summer breeding colonies of birds in both the Arctic and the Antarctic attract a number of predatory birds quick to enjoy the easy meals of eggs and chicks. In the Arctic, the small mammals of the tundra lands, such as lemmings and hares, increase the range of food for birds to hunt. The variety of predatory birds is therefore greater in the Arctic than in the Antarctic and includes eagles, skuas, owls, falcons, and buzzards. The predators time their own breeding cycle to coincide with that of their prey, to ensure that their chicks will always have plenty to eat.

GHOSTLY HUNTER
Snowy owls feed largely on the millions of lemmings living on the Arctic tundra. The owl population usually follows the rise and fall of the lemming population on its 3- to 4-year cycle (p. 36). Many of these superb owls wander far south in winter.

Soapstone and ivory owl carved by Inuit craftsman in Cape Dorset, Canada

Feathers at tips of wings spread out like fingers to help the eagle push and steer through the air

Spread feathers help the bird to reduce speed

Lethal curved talons grip, crush, and carry off prey

Broad wings give both speed and control in flight

Strong legs cushion impact of landing

The golden eagle slows in mid-air and spreads out its wings and tail to act as a brake

Eyes firmly focused on its destination, the eagle further brakes its flight by swinging out its lower body and legs

At the last moment, its feet swing down to grip the perch

WATCH OUT BELOW
Golden eagles fly at low altitudes while hunting, then swoop suddenly to pounce on their prey. This swoop-and-grab attack is effective because it happens so swiftly that the prey is often taken unawares. Here, a golden eagle is landing on a branch in much the same way as it would when diving for a meal.

KING OF THE CLOUDS
As the most powerful and majestic bird in the sky, the eagle features in countless stories, myths, and legends. Here, a magnificent eagle perches on a tree in an illustration by British illustrator Reginald Knowles. It forms the title page of a collection of Norse legends.

Golden eagle
Aquila chrysaetos

Sharp eyesight to spot birds and small mammals moving on the ground below

Hooked bill can tear flesh from prey

Huge chest muscles drive the enormous wings

Gyrfalcon
Falco rusticolus

Feathers down to toes to keep warm

BIGGEST AND BEST
The gyrfalcon, the most powerful of the falcons, relies on power and speed to catch its victims. It usually kills its prey in flight.

A KILLING MACHINE
A magnificent flier, the golden eagle is a fierce predator of ptarmigan and other birds as well as small mammals such as ground squirrels and hares. Its range extends widely across the Northern Hemisphere, and it even nests directly on the ground in tundra regions.

FALCON FOOD
The rock ptarmigan (*Lagopus mutus*) is the gyrfalcon's main prey.

Ocean wanderer

T HE HUGE, GENTLE ALBATROSSES of the Antarctic seas come ashore only to breed. They do not breed on the Antarctic landmass itself but on islands such as South Georgia that lie to the north of it. There are six species of albatross breeding in the Antarctic: the black-browed, grey-headed, yellow-nosed, wandering, sooty, and light-mantled sooty. Albatrosses raise only one chick at a time and the chick takes a long time to mature, sometimes remaining in the nest for up to a year. Chicks are protected from the intense cold by thick down feathers and an insulating layer of blubber, or fat. When winter begins, most albatrosses set off over the southern oceans once more.

A man weighed down by more than grief: albatrosses can weigh up to 12 kg (26 lb)

DEAD WEIGHT
Sailors believed albatrosses brought them good luck. In Coleridge's *The Rime of the Ancient Mariner*, the unlucky mariner is forced to wear an albatross he has killed.

Wings very long and slender for effortless gliding above the ocean

Black-browed albatross *Diomedea melanophris*

BUMPY LANDING
Landing is a difficult task for a bird so well adapted to flying over the sea. When albatrosses approach the nest site, they circle round several times, before putting their legs down, like the landing gear on an aircraft. But they often land with a bump.

Webbed feet held wide to push against the air and act as brakes

Grey-headed albatross *Thalassarche chrysostoma*

Large eyes indicate sharp eyesight necessary for spotting food in the sea

BIRD MAN
People have always wanted to fly like birds but this design for an early flying machine was no challenge to the albatross's mastery of the air. For birds, as with planes, take-off and landing are the most dangerous parts of flying. Like planes, albatrosses need a runway to gather enough speed for take-off. Without this, their enormous wingspan and body weight ensure that they remain earthbound.

Tube-shaped nostrils have glands at the base that excrete excess salt

Bill has razor-sharp edges and catches fish and squid

LIVING THE HIGH LIFE
Although grey-headed albatrosses weigh only half as much as wandering albatrosses, they still find it hard to take off, so they live on steep cliff sides and get extra lift from the strong winds rising up over the cliffs. Because of the harsh conditions, only half their chicks survive, a rate that is not unusually low for Antarctic birds.

FAITHFUL FLYING ACE

The wandering albatross has the greatest wingspan of any living bird. Its wing power enables the bird to cover as much as 500 km (300 miles) a day; it alights on the sea in calm weather to feed. Like all albatrosses, it comes ashore only to breed. The breeding cycle is exceptionally long, taking a year to complete. It therefore breeds only every 2 years. Breeding is preceded by an elaborate courtship display, in which the two birds dance face to face making a variety of weird sounds, and clapping their beaks together loudly. Wandering albatrosses usually pair for life. The most elaborate displays take place among newly formed pairs; old established partners are more discreet.

Wingspan may be between 254–360 cm (8 ft 4 in– 11 ft 10 in)

During courtship, the bird points its beak to the sky and moos like a cow

SECOND-HAND FOOD

Parent albatrosses feed their young by regurgitating (bringing up) the seafood they eat in the form of a sticky, oily mixture. This takes place when they return to the nest after many hours, or even days, fishing out at sea. Both adults and young can use this smelly and sticky oil in defence, ejecting it with reasonable accuracy over a couple of metres (6 ft) range. Predators, such as skuas, may be repelled by the foul smell or immobilized if the sticky oil saturates their feathers.

Mother feeds regurgitated krill to chick

Nest is lined with grass and feathers

Nest is about 30 cm (12 in) high

Strong legs and wide feet assist landing and swimming

Wandering albatross
Diomedea exulans

BARREL NEST

The black-browed albatross makes a raised nest of mud and straw among the tussock grass.

Penguin parade

MILLIONS OF PENGUINS gathered at their noisy summer breeding colonies make one of the most spectacular sights of the Antarctic. Only two species, the Adélie and the emperor, breed on the Antarctic continent itself, but the gentoo, macaroni, chinstrap, rockhopper, and king penguin all breed within Antarctic waters. Emperor and king penguins lay a single egg; the other species usually lay two eggs each year. Penguins are supremely well adapted for swimming in cold seas. Some of their adaptations, particularly the dense, waterproof feathers and thick fat layers under the skin, also serve them well on land. The penguins rely on the fat as a store of energy when they are looking after eggs and chicks and cannot get out to sea to obtain food for themselves.

Short beak has feathers along part of its length for extra warmth

SAFETY IN NUMBERS
Penguins breed in huge, densely packed colonies called rookeries. Some rookeries contain millions of birds.

A PRACTICAL PENGUIN
Adélies winter out at sea off the pack ice but march inland to their breeding colonies in October. They navigate partly by means of the Sun. Adélies usually return to the same mates and nest sites every year. They lay eggs in November, and by February the chicks go to sea.

Powerful oar-like flippers propel penguin through water

Stiff tail of pointed feathers used as rudder in water and support on land

Torpedo-shaped body allows the penguin to slice through the water

Oily feathers overlap like roof tiles, providing a waterproof layer for the thick down feathers beneath

MENACING PENGUIN
An evil penguin stars in the Oscar-winning British animated film, *The Wrong Trousers*. The treacherous penguin leaves a trail of havoc behind it as it attempts to remove a priceless jewel from a museum. Penguins are not, however, generally famed for their participation in diamond heists!

Adélie penguin
Pygoscelis adeliae

Short legs are set far back on body and steer while swimming

PADDED PENGUINS PARASCENDING
Tough feathers, flexible skin, and thick blubber protect these penguins from knocks as they hurl themselves on to rocky shores or ice floes.

King penguin *Aptenodytes patagonicus*

Rockhopper penguin *Eudyptes chrysocome*

Gentoo penguin *Pygoscelis papua*

MARK OF DISTINCTION
The main distinguishing marks of penguins are on the head and upper breast, so the birds are identifiable when they swim on the surface. They use their colours and head crests for species recognition and for courtship displays.

KING PENGUINS
Kings have golden-orange patches on their ears and bill. The long bill is useful for catching speedy fish and squid.

GENTOO PENGUINS
The pink bill of gentoos is dagger-shaped to catch fish and krill. Gentoos can swim at speeds of up to 27 kph (17 mph).

ROCKHOPPER PENGUINS
Rockhoppers have conspicuous yellow eyebrows which they use for courtship display. They are the smallest polar penguin.

PREDATION
Adult penguins need to defend their eggs and chicks from predators, such as skuas. In the oceans, penguins are prey to leopard seals, sea lions, and killer whales.

NOISY NESTERS
Chinstrap penguins are good climbers, using their beaks and sharp claws to reach nest sites in high rocky places. They are noisy and aggressive penguins. They often take over the nesting sites of Adélies or steal stones from one another's nests.

Black feathers form a "chinstrap" across white throat

Shallow nest hollow lined with stones and vegetation

Chinstrap penguin *Pygoscelis antarctica*

Emperors of the Antarctic

IN EARLY APRIL, when most of Antarctica's wildlife heads north, the emperor penguin begins its 100-km (60-mile) trek south to reach its traditional nesting sites on the pack ice. To reach the breeding colony, and to leave it, the birds must cover a huge area of pack ice in pitch darkness. In early May, the female lays her eggs and returns north to the open sea. The male then undertakes an incredible feat of endurance. During the icy winter, he incubates the egg on his feet under a flap of warm skin. This means that for 2 months, the male cannot feed, and may lose up to half his body weight. The female returns to feed the hatched chick in July. Emperors rear one chick each year but only about one out of five survives.

FEET HEAT
Chicks stand on the adults' feet until they are about 8 weeks old, hiding under a brood pouch, or flap of skin, for extra warmth and protection. Older chicks rely on their dense, fluffy feathers and the warm bodies of fellow chicks to keep warm, while their parents search for food.

TRULY MAJESTIC
The largest penguin, the emperor is about 1.15 m (nearly 4 ft) tall, and weighs 30 kg (65 lb). It can spend up to 18 minutes underwater and dive to over 260 m (850 ft).

Birds in the centre are the warmest of the group

A tightly packed group can reduce heat loss by as much as 50 per cent

Birds take turns occupying the most exposed position

Emperors tend to turn their backs on the constantly shifting wind

TOGETHERNESS
Incubating males huddle together for warmth, moving very little in order to conserve energy. When the chicks are born, the birds still huddle together as much as possible. Some emperor colonies contain over 20,000 pairs.

After the females have returned, the emaciated males make their way to the open sea

Penguin "flies" out of the water to draw breath

Penguin catches fish and krill in its beak

Underwater, penguin steers with its feet and tail

Penguin shoots onto land or ice in giant leap of up to 2 m (6 ft)

DUCKING AND DIVING
Penguins "fly" through the water propelled by their stiff flippers. When swimming fast, they often use a technique called porpoising, leaping out of the water like dolphins or porpoises. Air offers less resistance to movement than water, so porpoising penguins can travel at speeds of 30 kph (18 mph).

Bill is small to cut
down on heat loss

Emperor penguin
Aptenodytes forsteri

In the nasal
cavities, much
of the warm
air normally
lost in breathing
is recycled

Closely packed,
overlapping
feathers cover a
thick layer
of blubber

Feet are small
to cut down
on heat loss

King of the Arctic

THE POLAR BEAR IS ONE OF THE LARGEST and most powerful hunters of the Arctic; an average male weighs as much as six adult people. Polar bears are found across the Arctic region, and some even roam as far as the North Pole. They are solitary animals except in the breeding season. They do not hibernate, and in the long winter, when the sea ice is at its greatest extent, they hunt for seals coming up for air at breathing holes in the ice. Their dense fur keeps them warm even in the most severe conditions. An undercoat of thick fur is protected by an outer coat of long guard hairs. These hairs stick together when they get wet, forming a waterproof barrier. Under the fur, a thick layer of blubber performs two roles – insulating the bear against the cold, and acting as a food store to help the bear survive hard times.

The small, rounded ears lose little body heat

Polar bear
Thalarctos maritimus

HEAVYWEIGHT
An average adult male polar bear measures 2.5 m (8 ft) from head to tail and weighs about 500 kg (over 1,000 lb). The largest males grow up to 3 m (10 ft) in length and can weigh up to 900 kg (2,000 lb). Female polar bears are much smaller than the males.

Female keeps floor clean by covering it with freshly scraped snow

Air vent scraped in roof lets stale air escape

Female first digs the tunnel then hollows out the chamber

Pointed teeth capable of killing prey

BEARING ARMS
Play helps to strengthen cubs and lets them practise the skills they will need when they are adults. Young bears often wrestle in the snow with their mouths wide open to show off their sharp teeth. Such fights rarely result in injury. Finding and killing prey is hard and bears have developed a bad reputation for raiding human settlements in search of food.

CAVE CUBS
Polar bear cubs are born in December or January in a warm, cosy den dug in the snow by their mother. The cubs grow rapidly on their mother's rich milk, which is about 30 per cent fat. While in the ice cave, the mother has nothing to eat and lives on the stored fat in her body.

CAPABLE CLIMBER
In spite of their huge size, polar bears are quite able to climb trees, such as this one at Cape Churchill on Hudson Bay in Canada. Between 600 and 1,000 bears gather here in October to wait for the bay to freeze over so that they can head out over the ice to hunt.

Thick fur prevents bear from being scratched

Back legs are especially strong

POLAR PADDLE
Polar bears are very good swimmers. They swim slowly but strongly, and can keep swimming for days. They use only their front legs to swim, while the back legs are held still like a rudder.

SEAL SLAYER
Polar bears are clever and patient hunters. Over 90 per cent of their diet consists of seals. They wait by a seal's blow hole in the ice, pouncing as soon as it comes up for air. One stroke of the bear's massive paw and a bite at the back of the skull kills the seal. Most hunting trips are unsuccessful and a bear may not eat for 5 days.

White fur turns a little yellow in captive animals, such as this one

Hollow hairs trap warm air near body

Thickly padded soles covered by rough skin and sometimes tough hair

Sharp claws

Non-slip soles help grip slippery ice

The mighty moose

THE MOOSE IS THE LARGEST MEMBER of the deer family. It stands up to 2.4 m (over 7 ft) tall and can weigh up to 825 kg (1,815 lb). The moose can be found throughout northern Canada and the United States, and in northern Europe and Asia, where it is sometimes called elk. In Europe and Asia, the moose lives mainly in the coniferous forests bordering the tundra. In North America, some populations range widely over the tundra, spending long periods on the shores of the Arctic Ocean in mid-summer, when flies are likely to plague it further inland. When winters are particularly harsh, moose often move further south in search of food, to areas that have lighter snow cover. Moose are very solitary animals and their population density is low. Because of their immense size, they need a relatively large area to themselves to enable them to find an adequate food supply. However, in winter, when in search of new food supplies, they will often travel in a group, covering considerable distances.

Flat shape gives moose a stable surface with which to push rivals

The bell is a fold of skin covered with hair

LETHAL WEAPONS
The bull moose has heavy, flattened antlers. These are used for fighting rival males during the breeding season, rather than for protection. The moose sheds its antlers every year and grows a new set. By late August, the antlers are fully grown, and the bull strips off the "velvet" covering and polishes his great weapons against a tree.

Under surface of moose's foot

SURE FOOTED
The moose has long and sharply pointed hoofs, in contrast to those of its relative – the reindeer – which are rounded. The pointed hoofs help the moose grip the ice and snow.

Moose
Alces alces

Calf remains close to mother for several months

Reddish-brown coat becomes darker as the calf matures

Long legs allow even young moose to walk easily through deep snow

MAKING MORE MOOSE
The mating season of the moose lasts 4–8 weeks in the autumn. The bull wanders around looking for and calling females (cows); the cows return the calls. The bull will follow every sound to see if it was made by a cow or a rival bull. Baby moose are born in late May and June. The mother carries the baby for about 7½ months before the birth. There is usually one calf, although twins and even triplets are not uncommon. When the calf is about 10 days old, it can travel with its mother.

Antlers appear only in
males, and can spread to as
much as 2.05 m (6 ft 8 in)

Antlers are not
fully grown and
are still heavily
covered with velvet

MONEY MOOSE
The moose is such a revered
animal in many north
European countries that it
has even featured on
banknotes. This note
comes from Lithuania.

Muzzle hangs
8–10 cm (3–4 in)
over its chin

Short neck, coupled
with long legs, mean
that moose has to get
on its knees to eat
low-growing plants

SOLITARY GIANT
Within the tundra, the
preferred habitat of moose is
land that contains willow swamps
and lakes. Moose are fine swimmers
and can cross lakes and rivers with ease.
They like to roll in mud holes which helps
to get rid of any small parasitic animals. In
summer, they eat leaves and tender twigs,
as well as grass and herbs. Because of their
great size and dangerous antlers, they have
few natural predators, with the exception of
humans. Wolves may occasionally attack
isolated moose and young, although the
antlers of the male make it a formidable foe.

Arctic
willow
*Salix
arctica*

FAVOURITE FOOD
Arctic willow (*Salix arctica*) and
Alaska willow (*Salix alaxensis*) are
the favourite foods of the moose.

Moose is beginning to lose
the velvet on its antlers

WATER WADERS
Moose are often to be found standing up to their knees in
water. This helps them to get rid of the flies that trouble
them greatly in the warm summer months, but they also
feed on the aquatic vegetation. An adult will consume up
to 19.5 kg (43 lb) of vegetation a day. Sometimes, they
retreat into water to escape predators such as wolves.

Tundra mammals

THE ONLY LAND mammal that can live out on the Arctic sea ice is the polar bear. However, several mammals live on the Arctic tundra (pp. 8–9), either as residents or migrants. During summer in the Arctic, a great deal of the ice on the tundra melts, plants begin to grow, and insects hatch out. This means that there is suddenly plenty of food for animals that have spent all winter on the tundra, as well as for the migrants who arrive as soon as the weather warms. For much of the summer, the Sun never sets (pp. 6–7), therefore animals can feed around the clock. It is necessary for them to do this so that the young can grow as quickly as possible, because the summer is short and the land soon freezes over again.

TUNDRA VEGETATION
The tundra consists of a nearly continuous, though at times thin, cover of vegetation. Sedges such as the Arctic cottongrass (*Eriophorum angustifolium*, above) predominate, together with true grasses. Scattered among the grasses are various mosses, a variety of flowering herbs, and a few species of dwarf shrubs and willows.

Limit of permanent ice
Limit of drift ice
Tree line
Tundra

Arctic Circle
Canada
Arctic Ocean
Greenland
Russia

SEA OF ICE
The central area of the Arctic Ocean remains permanently frozen. The tundra, which spans North America and Eurasia is covered in snow and ice in winter, but is verdant in summer. No trees grow on the tundra because it is too cold and windy even in the summer months.

Long, pointed ears enable the lynx to hear well in dense, muffling snow

FELINE VISITOR
The Canadian lynx (*Lynx canadensis*) is mainly a creature of the forest that borders areas of the tundra in North America, but it is often to be found in the true tundra during the summer months. Its brown coat blends in well with the tundra landscape in summer, and in winter the coat becomes thicker and lighter so that the lynx is hard to see against the snow.

Snowshoe hare
Lepus americanus

Lemmings are very common on the tundra

HARE LINE
Three types of hare inhabit the tundra – the snowshoe hare, the rare Alaskan hare, and the common Arctic hare. Hares grow white winter coats and have well-developed claws that enable them to dig through the snow for food.

ACCIDENTAL DEATH
Every few years, driven by population pressures and food shortages, large numbers of lemmings try to migrate to new areas. Many drown while attempting to swim across broad rivers, but despite the popular belief, they are not trying to commit suicide.

In winter, big feet are covered with thick fur, which acts like a snowshoe

TURNCOAT
The stoat (*Mustela erminea*) is protected from harsh weather in its home beneath the snow. It is often called "ermine" when its coat is in its white winter phase. It is an attractive-looking animal, but a ruthless hunter. The stoat's slimness enables it to pursue lemmings, its main prey in the Arctic, through the lemmings' network of underground tunnels.

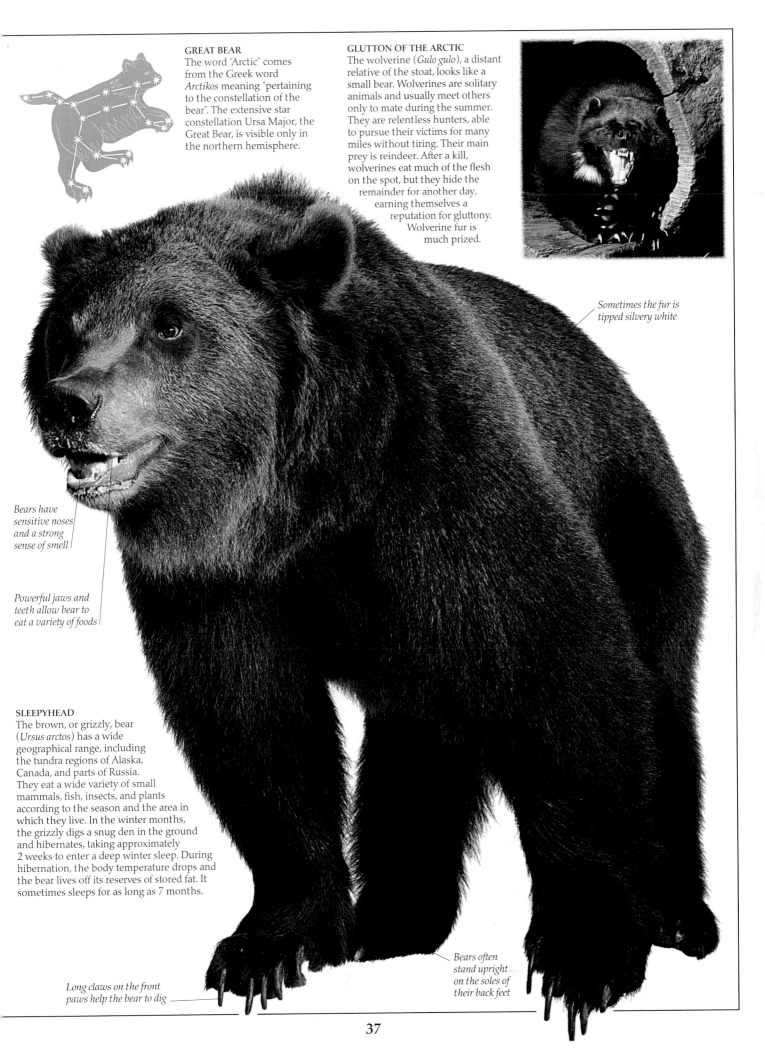

GREAT BEAR
The word "Arctic" comes from the Greek word *Arctikos* meaning "pertaining to the constellation of the bear". The extensive star constellation Ursa Major, the Great Bear, is visible only in the northern hemisphere.

GLUTTON OF THE ARCTIC
The wolverine (*Gulo gulo*), a distant relative of the stoat, looks like a small bear. Wolverines are solitary animals and usually meet others only to mate during the summer. They are relentless hunters, able to pursue their victims for many miles without tiring. Their main prey is reindeer. After a kill, wolverines eat much of the flesh on the spot, but they hide the remainder for another day, earning themselves a reputation for gluttony. Wolverine fur is much prized.

Sometimes the fur is tipped silvery white

Bears have sensitive noses and a strong sense of smell

Powerful jaws and teeth allow bear to eat a variety of foods

SLEEPYHEAD
The brown, or grizzly, bear (*Ursus arctos*) has a wide geographical range, including the tundra regions of Alaska, Canada, and parts of Russia. They eat a wide variety of small mammals, fish, insects, and plants according to the season and the area in which they live. In the winter months, the grizzly digs a snug den in the ground and hibernates, taking approximately 2 weeks to enter a deep winter sleep. During hibernation, the body temperature drops and the bear lives off its reserves of stored fat. It sometimes sleeps for as long as 7 months.

Bears often stand upright on the soles of their back feet

Long claws on the front paws help the bear to dig

Reindeer and caribou

Rᴇɪɴᴅᴇᴇʀ ᴀʀᴇ ᴄᴀʟʟᴇᴅ ᴄᴀʀɪʙᴏᴜ in North America. The name "caribou" may come from *xalibu*, the Native American Micmac word for "the animal that paws through snow for its food". Wild reindeer still survive on the frozen tundra of North America, Scandinavia, and Siberia, but they have also been domesticated in Scandinavia and Siberia for thousands of years. Although their thick coats insulate them against the Arctic cold, many populations migrate south in the winter to find food and shelter. As they travel, they grow a thicker, greyer winter coat. In summer, reindeer are plagued by hordes of insects, such as mosquitoes and warble flies, as they graze on the tundra meadows. Their main predator is the wolf. Reindeer are the only deer in which both sexes grow antlers.

REINDEER STAR
The most famous reindeer in the world is probably red-nosed Rudolph, the reindeer who leads Father Christmas's sleigh.

Antler buds appear two weeks after the old ones are shed

New antlers are covered by soft, thick velvet

Fully-formed antlers are bone-hard

TITLE FIGHT
In the autumn mating, or rutting, season, bulls with their antlers locked together, wrestle to decide which is the strongest. The winner of these contests collects a group of cows for mating and then defends his harem against all challengers.

BIG, BIGGER, BIGGEST
Antlers are shed each year. Bulls shed their antlers at the end of the year, while the cows wait until spring. New antlers grow rapidly and are fully grown by the start of the autumn rutting season.

Nuclear explosion

NUCLEAR POLLUTION
In 1986, a nuclear reactor at Chernobyl in the Ukraine exploded. Lichens and mosses absorbed radioactive Caesium-137 from the nuclear fall-out. Reindeer ate the lichens, which made them sick and their meat unfit to eat.

Reindeer moss (*Cladonia* species) absorbed radioactivity from the air

Velvet contains blood vessels to nourish the growing antlers

Reindeer or caribou
Rangifer tarandus

LICHEN LUNCH
Reindeer feed largely on lichens, which are one of the few foods available throughout the Arctic winter. Some reindeer living on Arctic islands will also eat seaweed. In summer, a wider variety of plants are available. Adult reindeer eat about 4.5 kg (10 lb) of food a day to get the energy they need.

Sensitive nose helps reindeer to find food even under the snow

CEREMONIAL APRON
This shaman's ceremonial apron was made from reindeer hide. The shaman was a powerful figure in the culture of many native Siberian and North American peoples. It was believed that he could draw power from the supernatural beings that were everywhere on land, and even lurked beneath the sea.

Iron symbols of the Sun, fish, and diving birds decorate apron

Heat is lost rapidly through antlers in velvet, cooling the reindeer on hot summer days

Hollow hairs contain air, which traps body heat

Muzzle covered with fine, warm hair

SWIMMING CHAMPIONS
Migrating reindeer have to cross many fast-flowing rivers. They are strong swimmers, plunging into the icy waters without any hesitation. The reindeers' broad feet help them to swim strongly against the current, and the hollow hairs in their coats help them to float more easily.

Iron-bladed reindeer skin scraper used by Siberian Tungus tribe

Lapp stick with spade-like blade to probe under the snow for food

TOOLS OF THE TRADE
Many Scandinavian and Siberian peoples relied on the reindeer for food, clothing, and shelter. They devised many tools specifically to enable them to take full advantage of their domesticated animals.

Dense, waterproof coat turns grey-white in winter

Broad feet fringed with fur stop reindeer sinking into snow

Sharp hoofs grip ice and dig through snow for food

GROWING UP FAST
Calves are born in June and grow fast on their mother's rich milk, which is four times as nutritious as cow's milk. Calves can keep up with the movements of the herd when they are 1–2 days old, and are better protected from predators such as wolves if they remain within its safety. Calves stay with their mothers for about a year, growing their first antlers when they are around 2 months old.

Company of wolves

WOLVES ARE INTELLIGENT, ADAPTABLE animals with a wide natural range. Arctic populations rely on their thick fur and cooperative hunting techniques to survive. They generally live in packs of between 8 and 20 family members. They are bonded together by affection for each other, and a ranking system of near military precision. Pack members establish their rank at almost every meeting: a dominant or high-ranking wolf stands erect, ears and tail pointing upwards, and may show its teeth, then growl. A subordinate or low-ranking wolf crouches, holds its tail between its legs, and turns down its ears; instead of growling, it whines. A wolf pack ranges over a specific area, picking off sick, aged, or injured herd animals. Needlessly feared and persecuted by humans for thousands of years, wolves kill only to survive and do not deserve their bad reputation – they are, in fact, the ancestors of all domesticated dogs.

BLENDING INTO THE BACKGROUND
In the Arctic areas of North America and Eurasia, wolves often have white coats for camouflage. Because their prey cannot see them easily, wolves can get very close undetected. In the forests to the south of the tundra, the wolves have grey or even blackish fur.

RING OF HORNS
Wolves are expert hunters and prey chiefly on large hoofed animals such as caribou, moose, and musk oxen. To defend themselves from a wolf pack, a herd of musk oxen form a tight circle, with the wolves on the outside and the females and young in the centre. By panicking the musk oxen, the wolves can break the circle and reach the calves inside. But, if a wolf is caught by one of the musk oxen's horns, it can be tossed into the air and then trampled.

Mouth remains wide open during howling

Grey wolf
Canis lupus

Wolf throws back its head in order to howl

IN HARMONY
An eerie howl in the night echoes through countless horror films, striking terror into the hearts of the audience. In fact, howling is simply one of the ways in which wolves communicate with each other. Wolf-speak ranges from whimpers and growls to complex facial and body expressions. Wolves howl in order to keep in touch with pack members, or to warn other packs to keep out of the area. If one wolf howls, the others join in, often harmonizing with each other. The variety of sound makes the pack seem bigger and more formidable.

LEADER OF THE PACK
The wolf's instinct for power and freedom has inspired countless writers. The American novelist Jack London (1876–1916) wrote his novel *The Call of the Wild* after spending a year in the Yukon Territory in Canada. It is the story of Buck, a domestic dog who turns wild and eventually leads a wolf pack.

Sensitive ears can track sounds up to 3 km (2 miles) away

Wolves have as many as 17 different facial expressions

Poor eyesight means wolf must rely on superb hearing and sense of smell

Long muzzle hides powerful jaws and teeth capable of killing prey and tearing flesh; 42 teeth include sharp canines, which grip prey

Grey wolf
Canis lupus

THE WOLF WITHIN
Jack London's novel *White Fang*, set in the Yukon in Canada, is the story of a wolf domesticated to become a pet. In practice, it is virtually impossible, and illegal, to keep wild wolves as pets.

BORN TO BE WILD
Wolves are well adapted to Arctic life. Their keen sense of smell and hearing are perfect for tracking down their prey. They have evolved strong bodies and long legs with which they chase down their quarry. Agile and graceful, they can jump up to 4.5 m (15 ft) and can leap upwards, sideways, and even backwards, like a cat. Just like dogs, wolves walk on their toes and have large pads with claws that do not retract. This allows them to run fast on flat ground while keeping their footing on rocks, ice, and other slippery surfaces.

Two-layered coat with soft, dense underfur and long, outer hairs keeps out the cold

Wolves can sleep out in the open tundra, although they often find a snow hole or a cave in which to shelter

41

The weighty walrus

Huge, ungainly, and enormously fat, the walrus, a close relative of seals, has superbly adapted to its Arctic lifestyle. A thick layer of blubber (fat) keeps the animal warm. Four flat flippers make the walrus an excellent swimmer, as well as allowing it to shift its heavy bulk on land. Female walruses give birth in the spring, usually on boulder-strewn beaches. The female usually produces a calf every other year, and cares for her young for about two years – twins are very rare. Walruses follow the seasonal advance and retreat of the Arctic ice, migrating as far as 3,000 km (1,860 miles) north every time. In the process, the animals must evade polar bears and killer whales – their greatest enemies other than humans.

WORLD-FAMOUS WALRUS
Lewis Carroll (1832–98) included a walrus and a carpenter in his famous story *Alice Through the Looking Glass*. They invite some oysters to walk with them, and then eat them. In reality, walruses eat mainly bivalve shellfish, such as mussels and clams.

THE CALL OF LOVE
Walrus courtship is an elaborate process. A male seduces a female with barks, growls, and whistles. If she is impressed by his love song, she will slip off with him and mate in the water. These two walruses are tenderly rubbing moustaches prior to mating.

Thick skin on neck and shoulders protects the walrus during fights

FURRY FRIEND
Just like the much smaller catfish, walruses have a row of coarse but very sensitive whiskers. The whiskers grow constantly to make up for daily wear and tear. The walrus uses this delicate moustache to search for invertebrates on the murky ocean floor.

Broad front flippers can support heavy body on land

Walrus
Odobenus rosmarus

HEAVYWEIGHT
Weighing in at around 1 tonne (2,200 lb), this formidable male walrus surveys his domain. Females are only slightly smaller – they tip the scales at 0.85 tonne (1,900 lb) Tusks can grow up to 1 m (3 ft) long.

AN INTIMATE ARRANGEMENT
Walruses are intensely sociable animals. During the summer, bulls and cows lie around on the land, packed together in large, noisy groups called pods. Keeping close conserves body heat, as well as making it harder for a predator to pick off an individual animal.

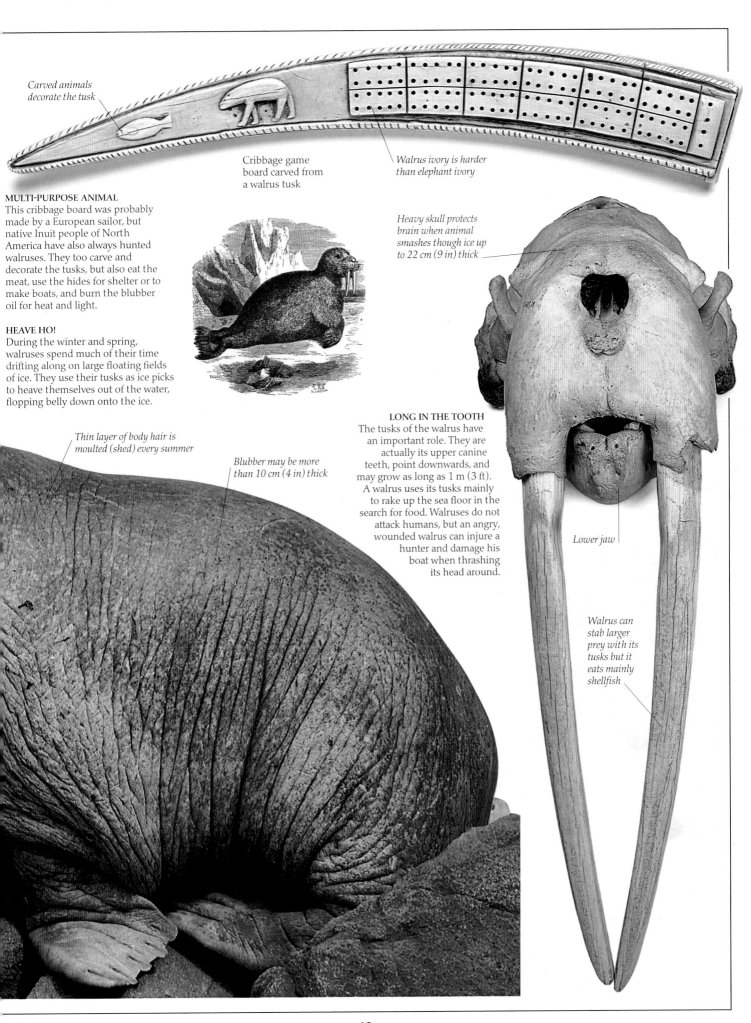

Carved animals decorate the tusk

Cribbage game board carved from a walrus tusk

Walrus ivory is harder than elephant ivory

MULTI-PURPOSE ANIMAL

This cribbage board was probably made by a European sailor, but native Inuit people of North America have also always hunted walruses. They too carve and decorate the tusks, but also eat the meat, use the hides for shelter or to make boats, and burn the blubber oil for heat and light.

HEAVE HO!

During the winter and spring, walruses spend much of their time drifting along on large floating fields of ice. They use their tusks as ice picks to heave themselves out of the water, flopping belly down onto the ice.

Heavy skull protects brain when animal smashes though ice up to 22 cm (9 in) thick

LONG IN THE TOOTH

The tusks of the walrus have an important role. They are actually its upper canine teeth, point downwards, and may grow as long as 1 m (3 ft). A walrus uses its tusks mainly to rake up the sea floor in the search for food. Walruses do not attack humans, but an angry, wounded walrus can injure a hunter and damage his boat when thrashing its head around.

Lower jaw

Walrus can stab larger prey with its tusks but it eats mainly shellfish

Thin layer of body hair is moulted (shed) every summer

Blubber may be more than 10 cm (4 in) thick

Suited to the sea

Seals are probably the hardiest of all the Arctic and Antarctic mammals. The ringed seal of the Arctic and the Weddell seal of the Antarctic both survive below the ice during the dark winter months. Other seals, such as the Arctic harp seal, migrate into polar waters as the warmer summer weather arrives. All seals have to leave the water to rest, give birth, and mate. In contrast to their graceful swimming in the sea, seals move clumsily on land, wriggling and sliding across the ice with some difficulty. Seals usually give birth in late winter. By spring, the pups are strong enough to start making the most of the fish and other rich food supplies of the polar waters. Fur seals and sea lions have problems coping with the heat of an Arctic or Antarctic summer. Their fur and blubber causes them to overheat, and the seals have to pant, flap their flippers, or cover their bodies with sand or mud to cool down. Seals have been hunted for their fur and blubber for hundreds of years; they are also threatened by the increasing pollution of the oceans.

Guard hairs protect the seal as it slides over rocks on land

Dense underfur traps a layer of warm air and keeps seal warm

TWO FUR COATS
Fur seals have two kinds of hair in their coat. Long guard hairs on the outside form a protective layer, while fine underfur stops body heat escaping. Many seals have hairless bodies, and depend on their blubber for warmth.

ICY WINTERS
Weddell seals (*Leptonychotes weddelli*) spend the whole winter under the Antarctic sea ice, gnawing at the ice with their teeth to keep open air holes for breathing. In summer, the seals move onto the ice or rocks. Pups are born in September and October and can swim at about 6 weeks. Weddell seals make a wide range of sounds under water, possibly for locating prey or breathing holes, or to communicate with other seals. They can dive to depths of about 580 m (1,900 ft) and stay submerged for up to 70 minutes.

BALLOON NOSE
Male hooded seals (*Cystaphora cristata*) of the Arctic have an inflatable balloon-like structure at the end of their nose. The seal inflates it when he is excited or in danger, and it may serve to warn off rivals or enemies.

The male has a huge swollen nose like an elephant's trunk

JOBS FOR THE BOYS
Gigantic male southern elephant seals (*Mirounga leonina*) roar defiance to their rivals in the breeding season, using their extraordinary nose like a loudspeaker. The female gives birth to a single pup, which she suckles for about a month. During this period, she will not feed, existing instead on energy reserves in her blubber. Males do not eat during the breeding season either, since they are constantly defending a harem of females against rival males.

Male elephant seals are up to 10 times heavier than females

While it is suckled, the pup may quadruple its weight in 3–4 weeks

HIDDEN DEATH
Inuit hunters sometimes hide behind white shields mounted on small sledges as they hunt seals.

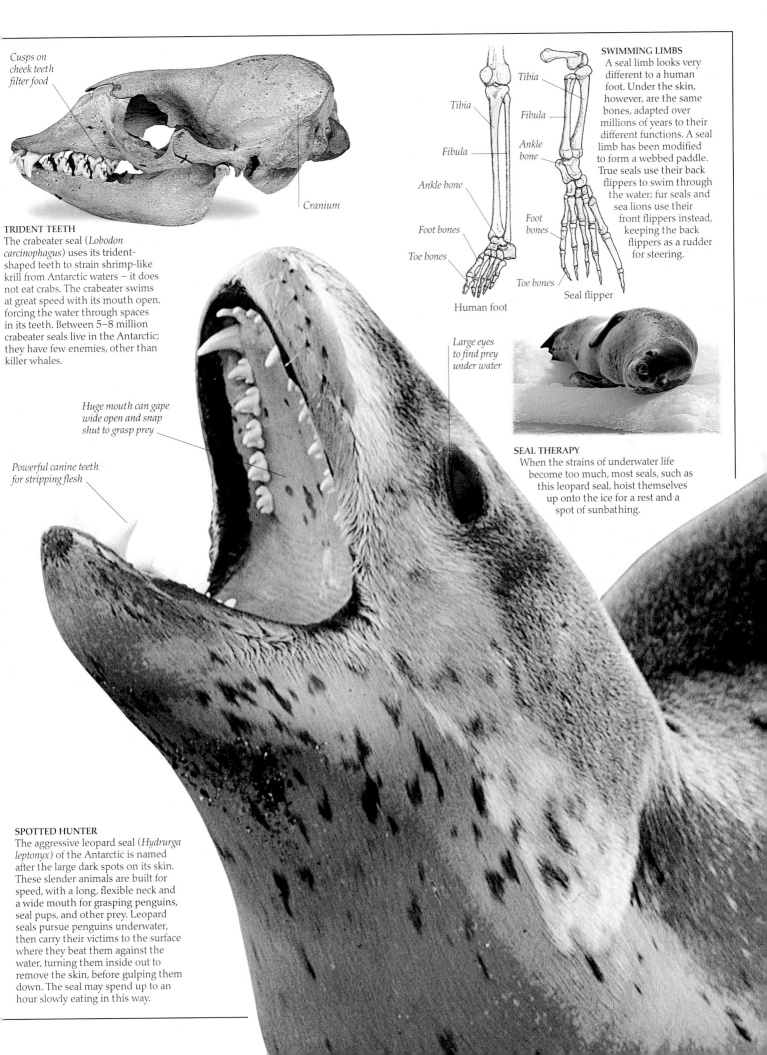

*Cusps on
cheek teeth
filter food*

Cranium

TRIDENT TEETH

The crabeater seal (*Lobodon
carcinophagus*) uses its trident-
shaped teeth to strain shrimp-like
krill from Antarctic waters – it does
not eat crabs. The crabeater swims
at great speed with its mouth open,
forcing the water through spaces
in its teeth. Between 5–8 million
crabeater seals live in the Antarctic;
they have few enemies, other than
killer whales.

*Huge mouth can gape
wide open and snap
shut to grasp prey*

*Powerful canine teeth
for stripping flesh*

SWIMMING LIMBS

A seal limb looks very
different to a human
foot. Under the skin,
however, are the same
bones, adapted over
millions of years to their
different functions. A seal
limb has been modified
to form a webbed paddle.
True seals use their back
flippers to swim through
the water; fur seals and
sea lions use their
front flippers instead,
keeping the back
flippers as a rudder
for steering.

Tibia

Fibula

Tibia

Fibula

*Ankle
bone*

Ankle bone

*Foot
bones*

Foot bones

Toe bones

Toe bones

Human foot

Seal flipper

*Large eyes
to find prey
under water*

SEAL THERAPY

When the strains of underwater life
become too much, most seals, such as
this leopard seal, hoist themselves
up onto the ice for a rest and a
spot of sunbathing.

SPOTTED HUNTER

The aggressive leopard seal (*Hydrurga
leptonyx*) of the Antarctic is named
after the large dark spots on its skin.
These slender animals are built for
speed, with a long, flexible neck and
a wide mouth for grasping penguins,
seal pups, and other prey. Leopard
seals pursue penguins underwater,
then carry their victims to the surface
where they beat them against the
water, turning them inside out to
remove the skin, before gulping them
down. The seal may spend up to an
hour slowly eating in this way.

Giants of the seas

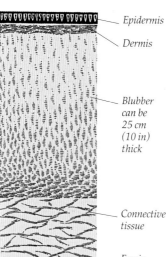

INUIT CARVING
This Inuit model of a sperm whale comes from Alaska. Whalers were much influenced by Inuit carving when they began to engrave the teeth and bones of whales.

THE POLAR SEAS are home to a whole range of whales. The grey, humpback, fin, and blue whales are summer residents, making good use of a rich supply of plankton. When winter comes, most of the whales migrate to warmer waters near the Equator. The narwhal, beluga, and bowhead whales remain in the Arctic all year round, while minke whales survive the Antarctic winter. Whales do not feed much during the winter, relying on body fat to sustain them. Whales began to disappear when people hunted them for profit from their oil, baleen, and meat. Now that commercial whaling has declined, many whale populations have recovered.

SEA UNICORN
The spiral tusk of the male narwhal (*Monodon monoceros*) is an elongated tooth. Tusks were traded before people outside the Arctic had seen narwhals and may have led to the legend of the unicorn.

Epidermis

Dermis

Blubber can be 25 cm (10 in) thick

Connective tissue

Fascia

Muscles

HOT FAT
Under a whale's skin there is an insulating layer of fatty blubber. A network of blood vessels runs through it. If the whale overheats, more blood is pumped up nearer to the cold water, which cools the whale down.

Blowhole on top of head; nostrils are closed off under water

Grey whale
Eschrichtius robustus

Barnacles often glue themselves to a grey whale's skin and hitch a ride around the oceans

ONE LONG HOLIDAY
Grey whales make the longest migration journeys of any whale. They winter off the coasts of California and Mexico, then swim to their Alaskan feeding grounds for the summer, a round trip of more than 20,000 km (12,000 miles). Grey whales only feed in the summer, living off stores of energy in their blubber for the rest of the year. The young are born in the warmer waters of their winter home.

BONEFINGER
Inside a whale's flipper are the same bones as in our own hands. Flippers are used for steering and braking; the tail gives the swimming power.

About 150 pairs of yellowish-white baleen plates filter plankton

46

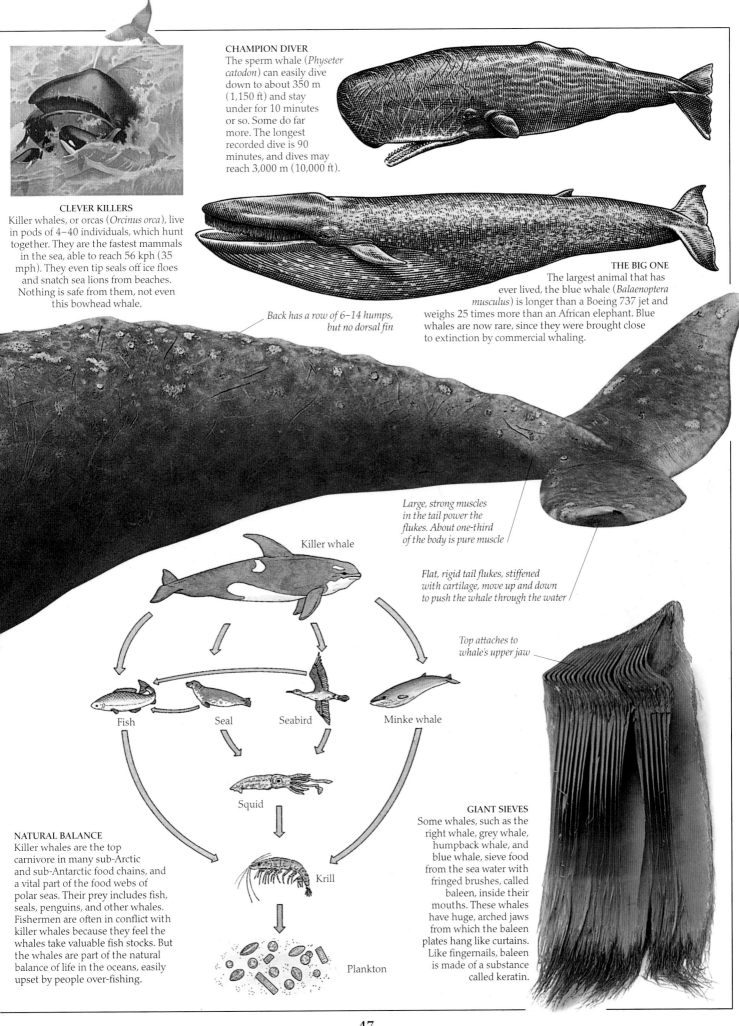

CHAMPION DIVER
The sperm whale (*Physeter catodon*) can easily dive down to about 350 m (1,150 ft) and stay under for 10 minutes or so. Some do far more. The longest recorded dive is 90 minutes, and dives may reach 3,000 m (10,000 ft).

CLEVER KILLERS
Killer whales, or orcas (*Orcinus orca*), live in pods of 4–40 individuals, which hunt together. They are the fastest mammals in the sea, able to reach 56 kph (35 mph). They even tip seals off ice floes and snatch sea lions from beaches. Nothing is safe from them, not even this bowhead whale.

Back has a row of 6–14 humps, but no dorsal fin

THE BIG ONE
The largest animal that has ever lived, the blue whale (*Balaenoptera musculus*) is longer than a Boeing 737 jet and weighs 25 times more than an African elephant. Blue whales are now rare, since they were brought close to extinction by commercial whaling.

Large, strong muscles in the tail power the flukes. About one-third of the body is pure muscle

Flat, rigid tail flukes, stiffened with cartilage, move up and down to push the whale through the water

Top attaches to whale's upper jaw

Killer whale

Fish

Seal

Seabird

Minke whale

Squid

Krill

Plankton

NATURAL BALANCE
Killer whales are the top carnivore in many sub-Arctic and sub-Antarctic food chains, and a vital part of the food webs of polar seas. Their prey includes fish, seals, penguins, and other whales. Fishermen are often in conflict with killer whales because they feel the whales take valuable fish stocks. But the whales are part of the natural balance of life in the oceans, easily upset by people over-fishing.

GIANT SIEVES
Some whales, such as the right whale, grey whale, humpback whale, and blue whale, sieve food from the sea water with fringed brushes, called baleen, inside their mouths. These whales have huge, arched jaws from which the baleen plates hang like curtains. Like fingernails, baleen is made of a substance called keratin.

A herding life

PEOPLE HAVE SURVIVED in the inhospitable Arctic regions of northern Scandinavia and the northern regions of Siberia for thousands of years. Native Arctic peoples followed a nomadic (travelling) hunting and fishing lifestyle, adapting to the intense winter cold, darkness, and snow without the aid of modern technology. Starvation and death by exposure were constant threats. Native peoples of the Eurasian Arctic include the Saami, or Lapps, of northern Scandinavia, and the Chukchi, Evenks, and Nenets of Siberia and northeastern Asia. Some families still follow reindeer herds, herding or lassoing them for their meat and pelts. Reindeer provided Arctic peoples with all their basic needs – food, clothing, tents, tools, and items to trade. In some remote areas, the native peoples still manage to follow a traditional hunting lifestyle. But many now work in villages or towns, with some combining the old and new ways of life.

Staff is made of iron

SPIRIT POWER
In many traditional Siberian societies, a specially trained *angakok*, or shaman, acted as the link between the supernatural and natural worlds. A shaman fulfilled many roles, from doctor and meteorologist to performer of miracles. This shaman's headdress is embroidered with reindeer hair.

Shaman's head ornament from the Ostyak-Nenet people of Siberia

HANDY IN WINTER
This ivory carving of reindeer pulling a sledge comes from central Siberia. Many Siberian peoples used reindeer as pack and draught (pulling) animals for carrying their household goods. Today, some reindeer herders hire out their reindeer sledge for transport during the winter.

Foot represents a bear's paw

IN A TRANCE
Shamans of the Tungus people, east of the Yenisey river in central Siberia, held this staff while meditating. The shaman often went into a trance and spoke with the voice of a spirit "helper".

PACK YOUR BAG
The northern Komi live to the west of the Ural mountains, in northwestern Russia. Traditionally, they filled this *patku*, or kit-bag, with clothes and other smaller items, and loaded it onto a baggage sledge when following reindeer herds.

Bag is made of stretched reindeer hide

Hide from different parts of the reindeer body provides the changes of colour in the decoration

MOVING CAMP
Because nomadic people often moved several times a year, their tents had to be simple and lightweight as well as sturdy. The tents were usually based on a conical framework of wooden poles, covered with several reindeer skins. The top of the tent was left open to allow smoke from the fire to escape.

Nenet tent, Siberia

A great deal of heat is lost through the head so a hood is vital for keeping the head and ears warm in freezing conditions

Seams are very finely stitched to make the garment as warm and waterproof as possible

Nenet child's hooded winter parka

HUNTER OR HUNTED?
This hooded jacket from the Aleutian Islands between Siberia and Alaska is made from strips of seal or walrus intestine, sewn together to make a waterproof garment. By dressing in the skins, fur, or body parts of the animals, the hunter was making an important point – he became part of the animal world around him by taking on the appearance of both the hunter and the hunted.

Reindeer gut was often used for sewing skins together

Mittens are sewn right into the sleeves for extra warmth and protection

Fur trim was decorative, but also protected against icy winds

ORIGINS OF THE PARKA
A traditional winter coat of the Nenet tribe of northern Siberia consisted of a thick, warm, long-sleeved jacket called a parka. The coat was sewn together from pieces of reindeer skin. The reindeer hide was worn on the outside; for the inner clothing, softer fur was placed next to the skin for extra warmth. Woollen undergarments provided added protection, and helped to trap body heat. Some people still wear traditional clothes, but most now buy winter clothes made of synthetic materials.

Hunters of the north

The model has a traditional hairstyle

Strips of white hide from underside of caribou are used as decoration

Both men and women wore sealskin boots called kamiks

Inuit clothes were often heavily embroidered

INUIT, INUPIAT, AND YUPIK PEOPLE, CALLED ESKIMOS by 19th-century Europeans, are the original inhabitants of the Arctic tundra of northern Canada, Alaska, Russia, and Greenland. About 100,000 of them still live there. They were nomadic hunter-gatherers. They lived near the coast in summer, building up food reserves for the winter. The rest of the year, they travelled, hunting caribou, seals, polar bears, and whales, and used every part of the animals they caught for food, shelter, clothing, weapons, and tools. Their society was organized in extended family groups, with each member carrying out a specific job according to sex, age, and status. Games, music, and storytelling helped to pass the long winter hours. Most Inuit, Inupiat, and Yupik people now live in permanent settlements, often combining a regular job with hunting trips.

WINTER WARMTH
This traditional man's winter costume is made of caribou skin. Women sewed the skins together with sinew and a bone needle, and sometimes decorated the clothes with beadwork or embroidery. Only the families of good hunters had clothes that they replaced each year. Poor families unable to get autumn caribou skins wore their clothes for more than a year, or had to make their parkas out of sealskins.

ANCIENT ART
Inuit carved elaborate animal figures out of walrus ivory, caribou antlers, and whale or seal bone. They used ivory bow drills as instruments. This Inuit carving of a woman standing on a seal comes from Baffin Island. Today, Inuit artists use modern tools and soapstone to make carvings for tourists.

Only the tiniest area is exposed to the freezing air

Hunter pulled on line attached to harpoon to haul seal out of the water

Fitted tray holds leather harpoon rope

Sealskin jacket protected hunter from icy Arctic winds

A seal bladder float was attached to any large catch so that it would float behind the canoe

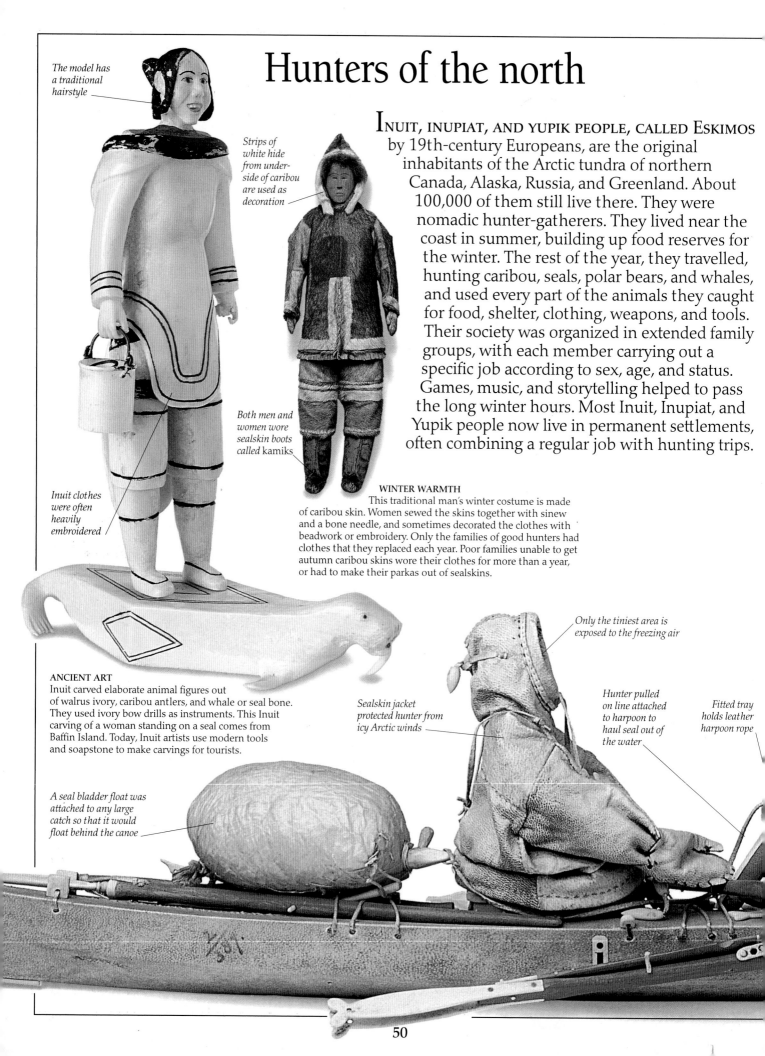

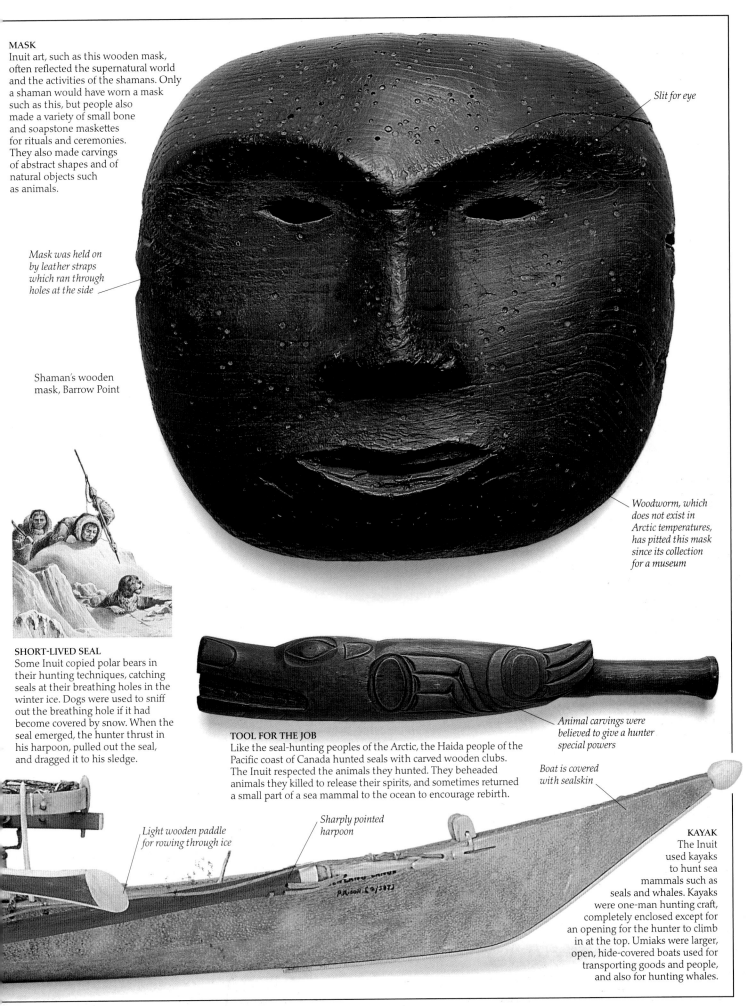

MASK
Inuit art, such as this wooden mask, often reflected the supernatural world and the activities of the shamans. Only a shaman would have worn a mask such as this, but people also made a variety of small bone and soapstone maskettes for rituals and ceremonies. They also made carvings of abstract shapes and of natural objects such as animals.

Slit for eye

Mask was held on by leather straps which ran through holes at the side

Shaman's wooden mask, Barrow Point

Woodworm, which does not exist in Arctic temperatures, has pitted this mask since its collection for a museum

SHORT-LIVED SEAL
Some Inuit copied polar bears in their hunting techniques, catching seals at their breathing holes in the winter ice. Dogs were used to sniff out the breathing hole if it had become covered by snow. When the seal emerged, the hunter thrust in his harpoon, pulled out the seal, and dragged it to his sledge.

TOOL FOR THE JOB
Like the seal-hunting peoples of the Arctic, the Haida people of the Pacific coast of Canada hunted seals with carved wooden clubs. The Inuit respected the animals they hunted. They beheaded animals they killed to release their spirits, and sometimes returned a small part of a sea mammal to the ocean to encourage rebirth.

Animal carvings were believed to give a hunter special powers

Boat is covered with sealskin

Light wooden paddle for rowing through ice

Sharply pointed harpoon

KAYAK
The Inuit used kayaks to hunt sea mammals such as seals and whales. Kayaks were one-man hunting craft, completely enclosed except for an opening for the hunter to climb in at the top. Umiaks were larger, open, hide-covered boats used for transporting goods and people, and also for hunting whales.

Discovering the Arctic

Norwegian flag

FROM THE 15TH CENTURY, European powers, intent on trade expansion, sponsored voyages into uncharted waters. Much of the early European exploration was centred on the search for a northern sea route to China and India which would halve the time and danger involved in travelling overland. After the discovery of America, two routes were envisaged: the Northwest Passage following the American coast, and the Northeast Passage, along the Siberian coast. The search for the Northwest Passage was soon monopolized by the British and the French, later joined by the Americans; the Dutch and the Russians concentrated on the northeast. Over the next 350 years, explorers opened up the Arctic, but it was not until 1878 that a Swede, Adolf Nordenskjïld, navigated the Northeast Passage, and 1905 when the great Norwegian explorer Roald Amundsen sailed through the Northwest Passage.

UP AND AWAY
Salomon Andrée, a Swedish aeronaut, and two companions, tried to reach the North Pole in the balloon *Örnen* (*Eagle*) in 1897. The balloon was weighed down by ice and forced to land. All three men perished.

Sir John Franklin, 1786–1847

Fox collar

RESCUE FOXES
Eight foxes were released in the Canadian Arctic wearing collars bearing the name and position of a rescue ship, and medals were distributed among the local people. It was hoped they might encounter Franklin survivors.

Medal

THE SEARCHERS
In 1845, Sir John Franklin led 128 men on a search for the Northwest Passage. By 1847 nothing had been heard from them, and his wife mobilized many expeditions to hunt for them. In fact, they had all died but the searches greatly advanced geographical knowledge of the Arctic.

THE HOMECOMING
In 1818, John Ross (leading the procession) returned home to England having failed to find the Northwest Passage but having succeeded in killing a bear! This cartoon was by George Cruickshank.

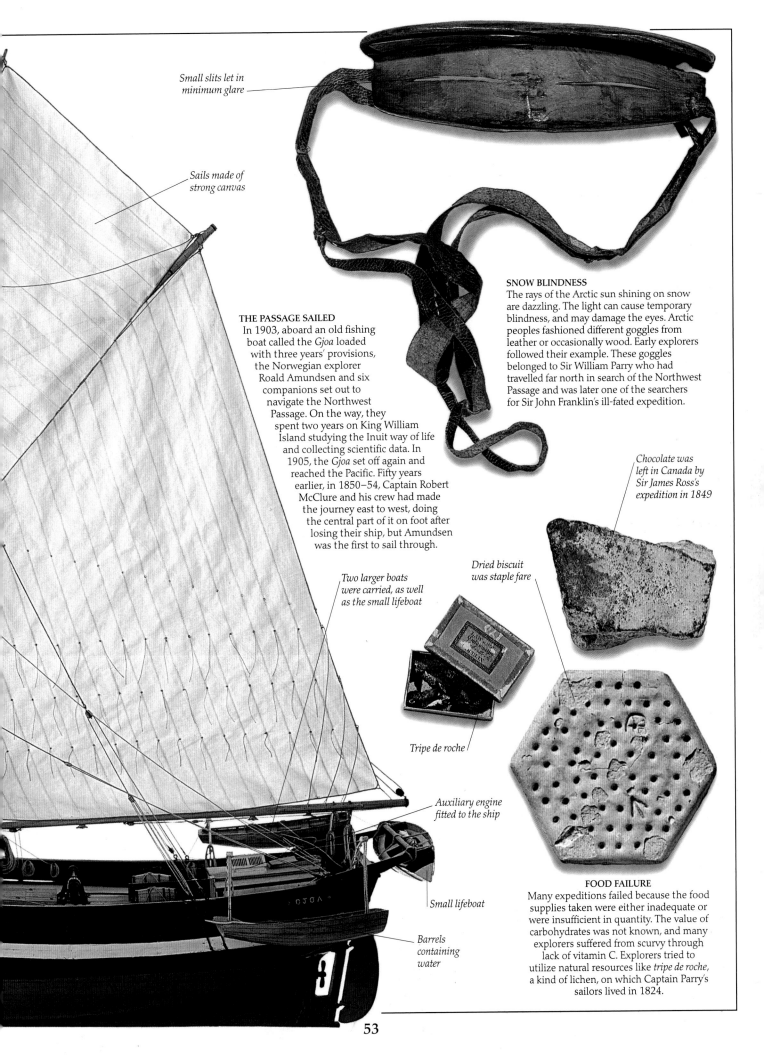

Small slits let in minimum glare

Sails made of strong canvas

SNOW BLINDNESS
The rays of the Arctic sun shining on snow are dazzling. The light can cause temporary blindness, and may damage the eyes. Arctic peoples fashioned different goggles from leather or occasionally wood. Early explorers followed their example. These goggles belonged to Sir William Parry who had travelled far north in search of the Northwest Passage and was later one of the searchers for Sir John Franklin's ill-fated expedition.

THE PASSAGE SAILED
In 1903, aboard an old fishing boat called the *Gjoa* loaded with three years' provisions, the Norwegian explorer Roald Amundsen and six companions set out to navigate the Northwest Passage. On the way, they spent two years on King William Island studying the Inuit way of life and collecting scientific data. In 1905, the *Gjoa* set off again and reached the Pacific. Fifty years earlier, in 1850–54, Captain Robert McClure and his crew had made the journey east to west, doing the central part of it on foot after losing their ship, but Amundsen was the first to sail through.

Chocolate was left in Canada by Sir James Ross's expedition in 1849

Dried biscuit was staple fare

Two larger boats were carried, as well as the small lifeboat

Tripe de roche

Auxiliary engine fitted to the ship

Small lifeboat

Barrels containing water

FOOD FAILURE
Many expeditions failed because the food supplies taken were either inadequate or were insufficient in quantity. The value of carbohydrates was not known, and many explorers suffered from scurvy through lack of vitamin C. Explorers tried to utilize natural resources like *tripe de roche*, a kind of lichen, on which Captain Parry's sailors lived in 1824.

Race for the pole

Surveying the land

At the beginning of the 20th century, several nations wanted to explore the Antarctic. In 1910, British adventurer Robert Falcon Scott (1868–1912) set out for the South Pole.

His expedition had scientific objectives. After using motor sledges, ponies, and dogs, and then hauling their own sledge through the harsh terrain, Scott and four companions, Wilson, Bowers, Oates, and Evans, finally arrived at the pole only to find that the Norwegian explorer, Roald Amundsen had reached it weeks before them. On the return journey, the weather worsened and, weakened by cold and hunger, all five men perished. But, although they lost the polar race, their scientific studies formed a new landmark in Antarctic science.

RUNNING REPAIRS
Dr. Wilson took this sewing kit on the ill-fated 1910–12 expedition. Keeping cotton and canvas clothing in good repair was essential in the harsh and difficult conditions.

Compact and lightweight kit for travelling

Microscope magnifies the image inside the instrument

Side mirror reflects light into the instrument

Günther & Tegetmeyer
BRAUNSCHWEIG, No 4716

BASE CAMP
From this desk in his "den" in base camp at Cape Evans, Scott wrote his diary, letters, and reports, studied maps, and planned the details of his trek to the pole. The extreme cold and the dry atmosphere have preserved the hut virtually as it was in 1910.

ELECTRIC SPIDER
This electrometer, taken by Scott to Antarctica, was used to measure minute fluctuations in atmospheric electricity. If there was a difference in electric charge between the Earth and the atmosphere, a small suspended mirror inside the electrometer would move. This movement was compared against the fixed line of a suspended fine filament from a black widow spider's web.

Wire to earth the instrument

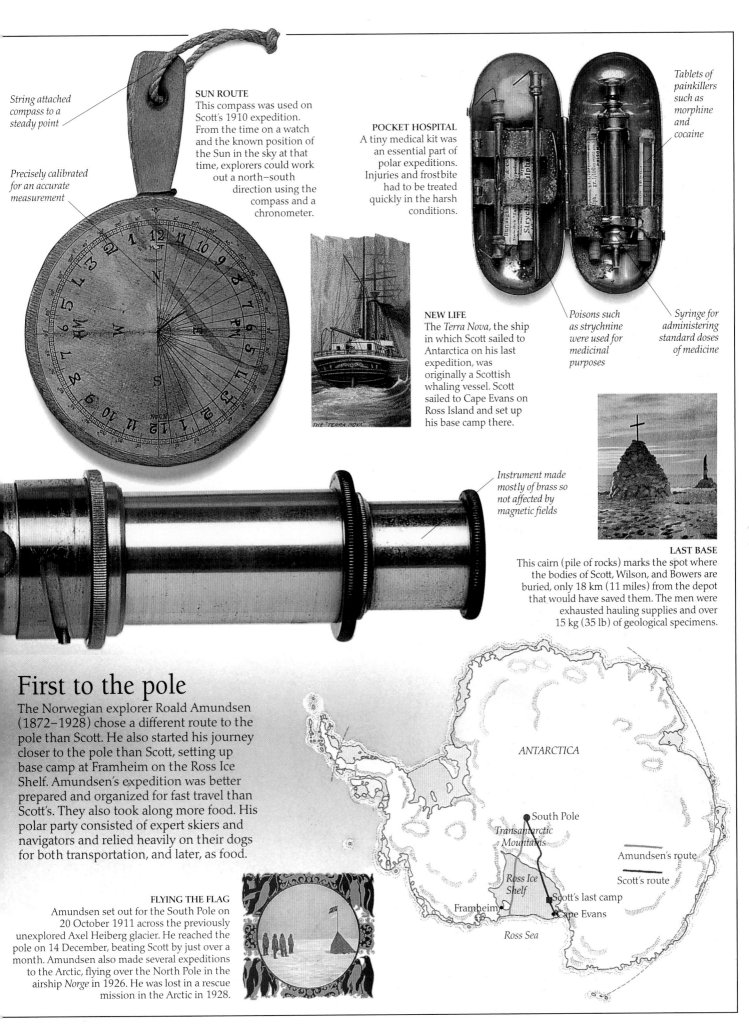

String attached compass to a steady point

SUN ROUTE
This compass was used on Scott's 1910 expedition. From the time on a watch and the known position of the Sun in the sky at that time, explorers could work out a north–south direction using the compass and a chronometer.

POCKET HOSPITAL
A tiny medical kit was an essential part of polar expeditions. Injuries and frostbite had to be treated quickly in the harsh conditions.

Tablets of painkillers such as morphine and cocaine

Precisely calibrated for an accurate measurement

NEW LIFE
The *Terra Nova*, the ship in which Scott sailed to Antarctica on his last expedition, was originally a Scottish whaling vessel. Scott sailed to Cape Evans on Ross Island and set up his base camp there.

Poisons such as strychnine were used for medicinal purposes

Syringe for administering standard doses of medicine

Instrument made mostly of brass so not affected by magnetic fields

LAST BASE
This cairn (pile of rocks) marks the spot where the bodies of Scott, Wilson, and Bowers are buried, only 18 km (11 miles) from the depot that would have saved them. The men were exhausted hauling supplies and over 15 kg (35 lb) of geological specimens.

First to the pole

The Norwegian explorer Roald Amundsen (1872–1928) chose a different route to the pole than Scott. He also started his journey closer to the pole than Scott, setting up base camp at Framheim on the Ross Ice Shelf. Amundsen's expedition was better prepared and organized for fast travel than Scott's. They also took along more food. His polar party consisted of expert skiers and navigators and relied heavily on their dogs for both transportation, and later, as food.

ANTARCTICA

Transantarctic Mountains

South Pole

Amundsen's route

Scott's route

Ross Ice Shelf

Scott's last camp

Framheim

Cape Evans

Ross Sea

FLYING THE FLAG
Amundsen set out for the South Pole on 20 October 1911 across the previously unexplored Axel Heiberg glacier. He reached the pole on 14 December, beating Scott by just over a month. Amundsen also made several expeditions to the Arctic, flying over the North Pole in the airship *Norge* in 1926. He was lost in a rescue mission in the Arctic in 1928.

Keeping warm and safe

EARLY EXPLORERS SUFFERED greatly because they did not know how to keep warm and dry in harsh conditions. The freezing power of the icy winds was also largely ignored. Frostbite was very common, and many men died of exposure. In time, lessons were learnt from the native peoples, and by the early years of this century, equipment had improved enormously. Explorers used sleeping bags and fur boots and wore canvas jackets to protect themselves from the icy winds. Provision of essential foods was another factor that blighted many early expeditions. On many early expeditions, too much emphasis was placed on the need for meat; and carbohydrates, vital for energy, were largely ignored. Today, a great deal is known about the foods necessary for a healthy diet.

FIGURE OF FUR
Amundsen's clothing was typical of that worn in the early 1900s.

LAYER BY LAYER
The inadequacy of the clothes they wore contributed to the deaths of Captain Scott and his companions. They sweated a lot – the sweat froze, making the body cold and the clothes heavy and uncomfortable. Layers of lightweight clothes would have allowed ventilation with the trapped air insulating against the cold.

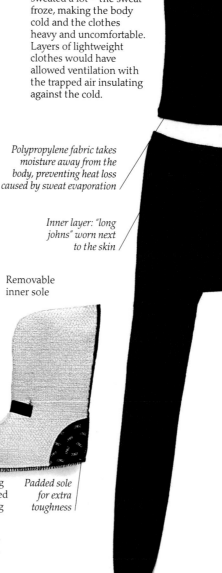

Polypropylene fabric takes moisture away from the body, preventing heat loss caused by sweat evaporation

Inner layer: "long johns" worn next to the skin

Potato

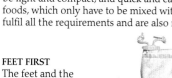

Bolognese sauce   Shepherd's pie

Cooking vessel

Removable inner sole

TRAVELLING LIGHT
Travelling in the freezing polar landscapes is hard work whether on skis, by skidoo, or sledge. Food, therefore, has to be light and compact, and quick and easy to prepare. Dried foods, which only have to be mixed with heated ice or snow, fulfil all the requirements and are also nutritious.

FEET FIRST
The feet and the hands are especially vulnerable to frostbite, so it is essential that these parts of the body are adequately covered. Today, different types of footwear have been designed for different conditions.

Thermal lining can be removed for easy drying

Padded sole for extra toughness

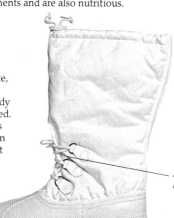

Adjustable lacing ensures a good fit

Glacier boots for use in deep powder snow

Thick, ridged rubber soles help prevent slipping

EYE SHADES
Goggles are worn to protect eyes from wind-blown snow and the glare of sunlight reflected off snow and ice.

Middle layer: fibrepile undergarment traps a layer of air, which is warmed by the body

ICE CRACKER
When climbing steep ice, two ice axes are banged into the ice face. The climber then uses them to pull himself up.

Zips allow garments to be easily removed

Waterproof nylon covering stops the goosedown becoming wet and losing insulating efficiency

Outer layer: jacket

Adjustable wrists prevent snow entering mitt

Thermal inner mitts are worn alone for delicate outside work

Waterproof outer mitts are lined with fibrepile fabric for warmth

POLAR MAN
One of the many advantages of layer dressing is that the number of layers can be adjusted according to the temperature and the activity of the wearer. This outer layer consisting of jacket and salopettes is filled with high-quality pure goosedown, which is the most efficient of natural fillings. Combined with the middle and base layers, these garments provide insulation sufficient to keep warm at -40° C (-40° F).

Outer layer: salopettes (thick, padded trousers)

Crampons attached to the soles provide grip

FOOT SUPPORT
These climbing boots are made of strong and fairly stiff plastic which supports the foot and ankle. They have a removable thermal lining.

Thermal socks worn next to the skin

Padded socks add extra warmth and help keep the feet dry

Polar travel

The snow and ice of polar regions have always posed special problems for travellers. Snow shoes and skis stop people sinking too far into soft snow, while boots with rough or spiked soles grip icy ground. Long, low sledges on smooth runners reduce friction and make it easier to move heavy loads over slippery, frozen surfaces. Early polar explorers learned from native Arctic peoples the benefits of using husky dogs to pull their sledges (Nomadic Lapp people used reindeer for the same purpose). Modern motorised vehicles, such as the snowcat, with claw-like grips, or the skidoo, with skis underneath, were developed from tried and tested traditional forms of transport.

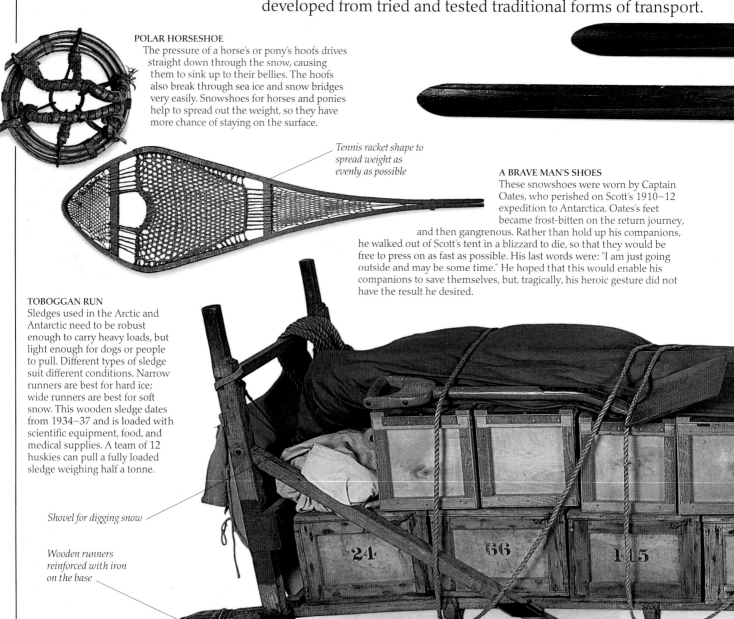

THE FIRST SNOWMOBILE
Scott's motorised sledge was the first vehicle with caterpillar tracks to be designed specially for snow. The slats on the tracks helped to grip the snow. The vehicle was far ahead of its time, but had an unreliable early petrol engine, and soon developed serious mechanical faults in the severe Antarctic environment. But it was a forerunner of the snowmobiles of today.

POLAR HORSESHOE
The pressure of a horse's or pony's hoofs drives straight down through the snow, causing them to sink up to their bellies. The hoofs also break through sea ice and snow bridges very easily. Snowshoes for horses and ponies help to spread out the weight, so they have more chance of staying on the surface.

Tennis racket shape to spread weight as evenly as possible

A BRAVE MAN'S SHOES
These snowshoes were worn by Captain Oates, who perished on Scott's 1910–12 expedition to Antarctica. Oates's feet became frost-bitten on the return journey, and then gangrenous. Rather than hold up his companions, he walked out of Scott's tent in a blizzard to die, so that they would be free to press on as fast as possible. His last words were: "I am just going outside and may be some time." He hoped that this would enable his companions to save themselves, but, tragically, his heroic gesture did not have the result he desired.

TOBOGGAN RUN
Sledges used in the Arctic and Antarctic need to be robust enough to carry heavy loads, but light enough for dogs or people to pull. Different types of sledge suit different conditions. Narrow runners are best for hard ice; wide runners are best for soft snow. This wooden sledge dates from 1934–37 and is loaded with scientific equipment, food, and medical supplies. A team of 12 huskies can pull a fully loaded sledge weighing half a tonne.

Shovel for digging snow

Wooden runners reinforced with iron on the base

Flat-bottomed sledge like a toboggan "floats" easily over the surface of the snow without sinking in too far

A RARE SIGHT
When Lapp people lived as nomads, migrating from place to place, they used reindeer as pack animals or to pull sledges. Today they rarely do so, because most Lapp families have settled in villages, although they still keep reindeer.

CANOEING THE SNOW
Traditional methods of travel in Lapland included various types of canoe-shaped sledge called *pulkkas*. These had one runner only and were usually pulled by reindeer. A common kind of *pulkka* was large enough for one adult passenger who sat with their legs outstretched, ready for braking. A wider *pulkka* was used to transport belongings. A third kind of *pulkka* was used by the Skolt Lapps for carrying sick people, children, and belongings. Reindeer were harnessed three abreast to this *pulkka*.

SMOOTH MOVERS
These heavy, wooden skis were used by Scott on his first expedition to Antarctica in 1901–04. Skis can be used on most kinds of snow and ice. They spread out the weight of a person, helping them to stay on the surface of the snow. They also reduce friction, sliding easily over snow and ice and allowing greater distances to be covered than by walking.

Stout wooden cases loaded with scientific equipment, food, and medical supplies

Canvas cover for protecting supplies

SNOW DOGS
The husky dogs used to pull sledges are social animals, working in a strict hierarchy under their leader in a sledge team. They are hardy, strong, and intelligent, but compulsive fighters. Huskies can survive freezing temperatures curled up in snowdrifts. The snow acts as an insulating blanket, helping to keep them warm at night or during blizzards.

DRIVEN TO THE DOGS
Sledges pulled by dogs are one of the best means of moving heavy loads over ice and snow. Normally, it takes at least a year or two of hard practice to learn how to drive a dog sledge.

Life at the poles

THE CRUEL SEAS, savage, unpredictable climates, and inhospitable terrains of the two polar regions have ensured that neither environment has ever been completely conquered by humans. Indeed, the history of polar exploration is one of appalling hardship and a terrible toll of human life. However, in the Arctic, the Inuit peoples evolved survival skills over the centuries, which enabled them to live a fruitful existence. European explorers learned much from their way of life and gradually applied this knowledge to their own ability to live in and explore these harsh environments. Today, the lifestyle at the poles for both Inuit and other polar dwellers is very similar. Scientific advances in clothing, transport, food, and building have ensured a way of life far removed from the hardships of earlier times.

HELPING HANDS
Many early explorers died because they could not build strong enough shelters. By the 19th century, Arctic explorers realized how much they could learn from the native peoples.

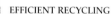

EFFICIENT RECYCLING
On Scott's last expedition, Edward Wilson made a successful candlestick out of a biscuit tin. Explorers tried to find an alternative use for everything.

Storage alcove

Window made from a block of freshwater ice

Entrance passage

OVERNIGHT STAY
Today Inuit may still build igloos as temporary shelter. Here, this hunter is lighting his primus stove with which he will warm himself and cook his dinner.

SNOW HOUSE
Contrary to popular belief, Inuit never built igloos as permanent homes but as temporary bases during the winter seal-hunting season. For much of the time, they lived partly underground in dwellings made on a frame of driftwood or whalebone and covered by turf.

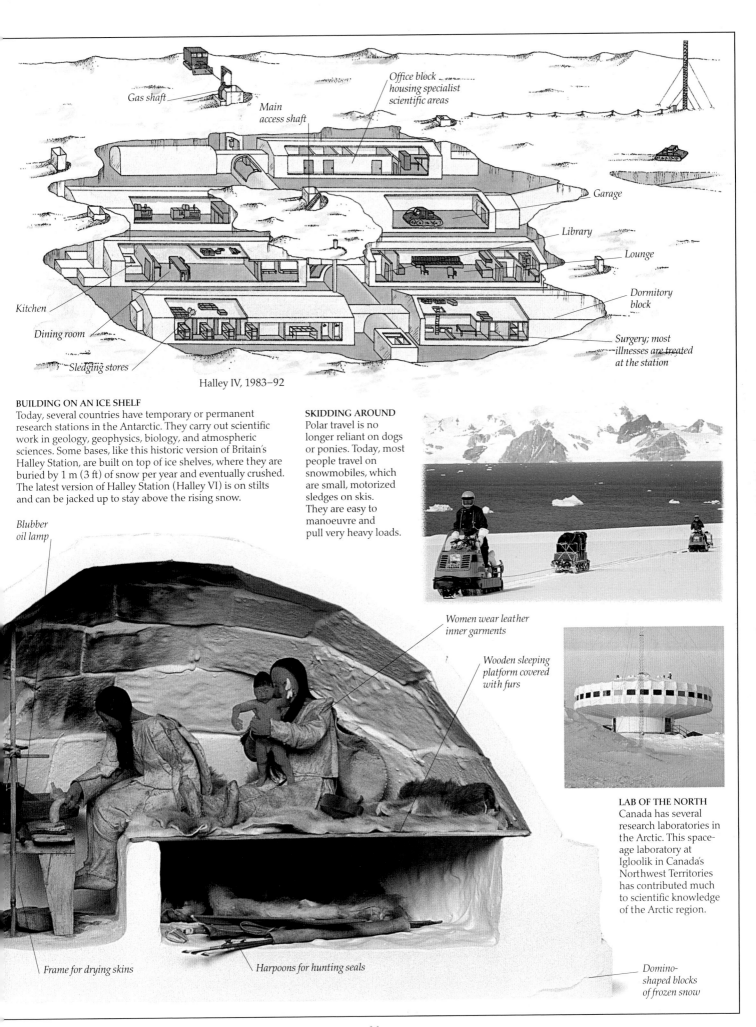

Gas shaft

Office block housing specialist scientific areas

Main access shaft

Garage

Library

Lounge

Dormitory block

Kitchen

Dining room

Surgery; most illnesses are treated at the station

Sledging stores

Halley IV, 1983–92

BUILDING ON AN ICE SHELF
Today, several countries have temporary or permanent research stations in the Antarctic. They carry out scientific work in geology, geophysics, biology, and atmospheric sciences. Some bases, like this historic version of Britain's Halley Station, are built on top of ice shelves, where they are buried by 1 m (3 ft) of snow per year and eventually crushed. The latest version of Halley Station (Halley VI) is on stilts and can be jacked up to stay above the rising snow.

SKIDDING AROUND
Polar travel is no longer reliant on dogs or ponies. Today, most people travel on snowmobiles, which are small, motorized sledges on skis. They are easy to manoeuvre and pull very heavy loads.

Blubber oil lamp

Women wear leather inner garments

Wooden sleeping platform covered with furs

LAB OF THE NORTH
Canada has several research laboratories in the Arctic. This space-age laboratory at Igloolik in Canada's Northwest Territories has contributed much to scientific knowledge of the Arctic region.

Frame for drying skins

Harpoons for hunting seals

Domino-shaped blocks of frozen snow

Last frontiers

At THE HEIGHT OF SUMMER in the Antarctic, tourist ships move gently around the coast. In the past, such sights would have been unthinkable, but today, people are willing to pay large amounts of money to see the last real wilderness in the world. In the Arctic, careless human exploitation in the past has damaged the fragile ecosystem. However, today, concerned governments are trying to find ways to develop the region while caring for the very special natural environment. Because the Antarctic is less accessible than the Arctic, it is still largely undamaged by humans, although holes in the ozone layer above the Antarctic have already been discovered. Many people believe that one way to preserve the area is to make the whole region into a world park, with any form of exploitation internationally banned. It is important to conserve the Arctic and Antarctic so that future generations can experience these extraordinary environments with their unique wildlife in their natural state.

DAY TRIPPERS
Tourist visits to the Antarctic have to be carefully monitored and organized, as tourists could damage fragile vegetation and disturb nesting and breeding grounds. On the other hand, tourist visits can help to spread concern for conservation.

RUBBISH DISPOSAL
The way people dispose of their rubbish in the Arctic and Antarctic often pollutes or damages the environment. Rubbish dumps on the edge of Churchill in Canada attract polar bears which can be poisoned or injured by eating the rubbish. The bears' nearness also causes fears for people's safety.

All snowflakes have six points

LANDS OF SNOW
The permanence of snow and ice in the Arctic and Antarctic regions is what makes them unique. Snow reflects back the Sun's rays, helping to keep temperatures low at all times.

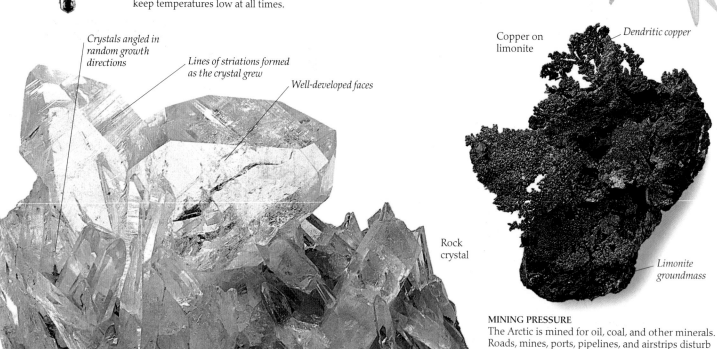

Crystals angled in random growth directions

Lines of striations formed as the crystal grew

Well-developed faces

Copper on limonite

Dendritic copper

Rock crystal

Limonite groundmass

MINING PRESSURE
The Arctic is mined for oil, coal, and other minerals. Roads, mines, ports, pipelines, and airstrips disturb wildlife and damage the fragile ecosystem. Several minerals have already been found in the Antarctic but the costs of exploiting them – together with increasing pressure to protect the environment – have led the Antarctic Treaty nations to agree to ban mining until 2041.

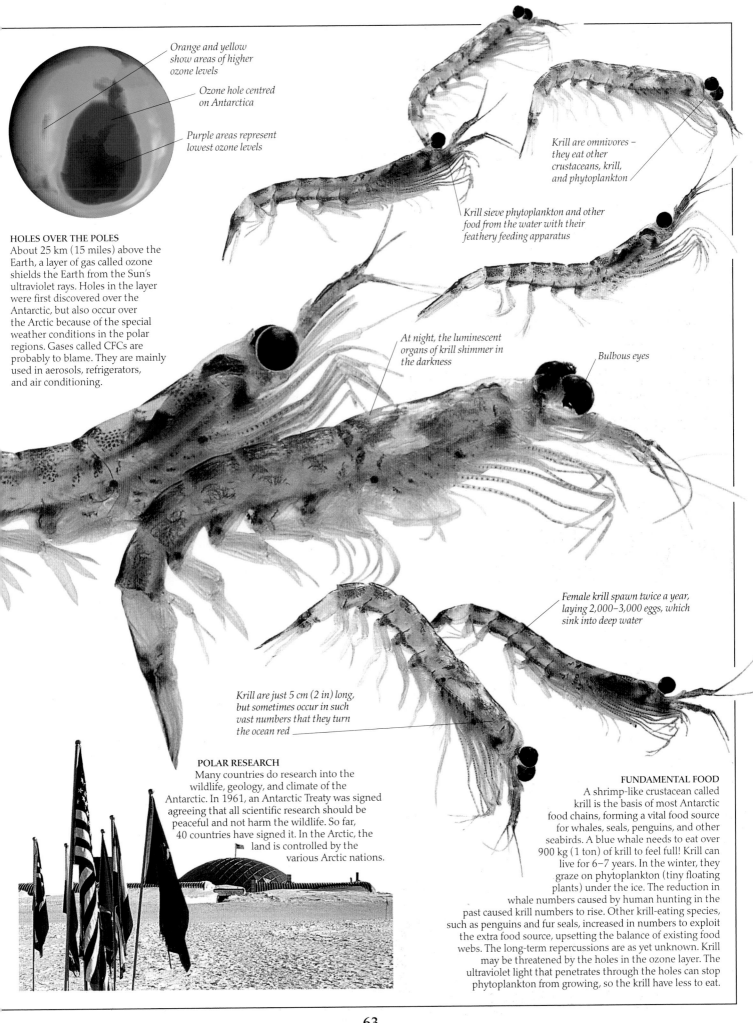

Orange and yellow show areas of higher ozone levels

Ozone hole centred on Antarctica

Purple areas represent lowest ozone levels

HOLES OVER THE POLES

About 25 km (15 miles) above the Earth, a layer of gas called ozone shields the Earth from the Sun's ultraviolet rays. Holes in the layer were first discovered over the Antarctic, but also occur over the Arctic because of the special weather conditions in the polar regions. Gases called CFCs are probably to blame. They are mainly used in aerosols, refrigerators, and air conditioning.

Krill are omnivores – they eat other crustaceans, krill, and phytoplankton

Krill sieve phytoplankton and other food from the water with their feathery feeding apparatus

At night, the luminescent organs of krill shimmer in the darkness

Bulbous eyes

Female krill spawn twice a year, laying 2,000–3,000 eggs, which sink into deep water

Krill are just 5 cm (2 in) long, but sometimes occur in such vast numbers that they turn the ocean red

POLAR RESEARCH

Many countries do research into the wildlife, geology, and climate of the Antarctic. In 1961, an Antarctic Treaty was signed agreeing that all scientific research should be peaceful and not harm the wildlife. So far, 40 countries have signed it. In the Arctic, the land is controlled by the various Arctic nations.

FUNDAMENTAL FOOD

A shrimp-like crustacean called krill is the basis of most Antarctic food chains, forming a vital food source for whales, seals, penguins, and other seabirds. A blue whale needs to eat over 900 kg (1 ton) of krill to feel full! Krill can live for 6–7 years. In the winter, they graze on phytoplankton (tiny floating plants) under the ice. The reduction in whale numbers caused by human hunting in the past caused krill numbers to rise. Other krill-eating species, such as penguins and fur seals, increased in numbers to exploit the extra food source, upsetting the balance of existing food webs. The long-term repercussions are as yet unknown. Krill may be threatened by the holes in the ozone layer. The ultraviolet light that penetrates through the holes can stop phytoplankton from growing, so the krill have less to eat.

Mapping Antarctica

ANTARCTICA IS A HUGE ISOLATED CONTINENT almost entirely covered by ice, where no plants can grow. The thickness of the ice means that on average, its surface is the highest of all the world's continents. Currents and strong winds sweep around the surrounding oceans, acting as a natural barrier between Antarctica and the rest of the world, and helping to keep it much colder than the Arctic. Cold sea water also drifts northwards from the continent, so that its cooling influence extends far beyond the Antarctic Circle. The southernmost Atlantic, Pacific, and Indian oceans together form what is sometimes called the Southern Ocean, surrounding Antarctica. Islands in this ocean provide breeding grounds for millions of seabirds attracted by the Antarctic's marine riches.

Key to map symbols

- ● Capital city
- ○ Settlement
- ◎ Scientific research station
- ▲ Mountain
- Glacier
- ⋯ Average limit of continuous sea ice
- ⋯ Limit of summer pack ice
- ⋯ Limit of winter pack ice
- → Warm current
- → Cold current
- ▦ Tundra

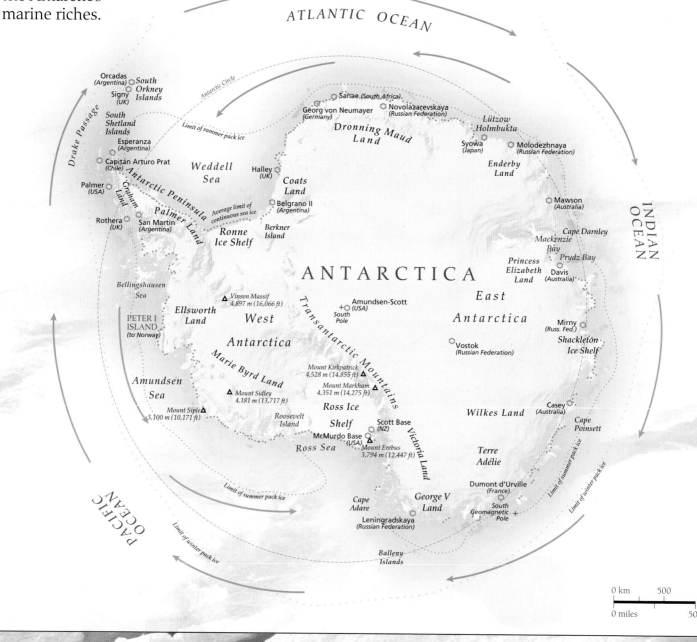

ATLANTIC OCEAN

Antarctic Circle

Orcadas (Argentina)
South Orkney Islands
Signy (UK)
South Shetland Islands
Esperanza (Argentina)
Capitán Arturo Prat (Chile)
Palmer (USA)
Rothera (UK)
San Martín (Argentina)

Drake Passage

Limit of summer pack ice

Sanae (South Africa)
Georg von Neumayer (Germany)
Novolazarevskaya (Russian Federation)

Lützow Holmbukta
Syowa (Japan)
Molodezhnaya (Russian Federation)

Dronning Maud Land

Enderby Land

Weddell Sea
Halley (UK)
Coats Land
Belgrano II (Argentina)
Berkner Island
Ronne Ice Shelf

Antarctic Peninsula
Graham Land
Palmer Land

Average limit of continuous sea ice

Mawson (Australia)

Cape Darnley
Mackenzie Bay
Prydz Bay
Princess Elizabeth Land
Davis (Australia)

ANTARCTICA

Bellingshausen Sea

PETER I ISLAND (to Norway)

Ellsworth Land

Vinson Massif 4,897 m (16,066 ft)

West Antarctica

Transantarctic Mountains

Amundsen-Scott (USA)
South Pole

East Antarctica

Mirny (Russ. Fed.)

Vostok (Russian Federation)

Shackleton Ice Shelf

Marie Byrd Land

Amundsen Sea

Mount Sidley 4,181 m (13,717 ft)

Mount Siple 3,100 m (10,171 ft)

Roosevelt Island

Mount Kirkpatrick 4,528 m (14,855 ft)

Mount Markham 4,351 m (14,275 ft)

Ross Ice Shelf

Scott Base (NZ)
McMurdo Base (USA)
Mount Erebus 3,794 m (12,447 ft)

Ross Sea

Victoria Land

Wilkes Land

Casey (Australia)
Cape Poinsett

Terre Adélie

Cape Adare
Leningradskaya (Russian Federation)

George V Land

Dumont d'Urville (France)
South Geomagnetic Pole

Limit of summer pack ice
Limit of winter pack ice

Balleny Islands

PACIFIC OCEAN

Limit of winter pack ice

INDIAN OCEAN

0 km   500
0 miles   500

64

Mapping the Arctic

THE ARCTIC IS LESS ISOLATED than the Antarctic, since the northern continents extend well inside the Arctic Circle. Much of the deep Arctic Ocean is covered by permanent pack ice, which is slowly rotated by ocean currents. The biggest area of land ice, though much smaller than Antarctica, is the Greenland Ice Sheet. Warm currents from the Atlantic Ocean mean that the Arctic seas north of Europe stay more free of ice than elsewhere.

Arctic Circle · **North Pole**

Spin of the Earth

Sunlight

Antarctic Circle

Axis of rotation

South Pole · Atmosphere

EXTREME SEASONS
The poles experience extreme seasons due to the Earth's tilt towards the Sun. Earth spins at an angle, so whether the North or South pole is tilted towards the Sun depends on the time of year. The diagram above shows the southern midsummer, when the whole area within the Antarctic Circle is receiving 24-hour daylight, while the Arctic lies in winter darkness.

Provideniya
Lavrentiya
Arctic Circle
Bering Strait
Chukchi Sea
ALASKA (to USA)
Ostrov Vrangelya
Wrangel Island
Northeast Station
East Siberian Sea
Toolik
Barrow
Limit of summer pack ice
Average limit of continuous sea ice
Inuvik
Amundsen Gulf
Beaufort Sea
Novosibirskiye Ostrova
Samoylov
RUSSIAN FEDERATION
Daring Lake
Banks Island
Victoria Island
Laptev Sea
Melville Island
ARCTIC
North Geomagnetic Pole
CANADA
Queen
Resolute Bay
Elizabeth Islands
Axel Heiberg Island
Eureka
Ellesmere Island
Grise Fiord
Alert
Igloolik
Lancaster Sound
Nares Strait
Lincoln Sea
North Pole
OCEAN
Average limit of continuous sea ice
Severnaya Zemlya
Franz Josef Land
Kara Sea
Willem Barentz
Thule
Knud Rasmussen Land
Kap Morris Jesup
Baffin Bay
Wandel Sea
Ny-Ålesund (France, Germany, Italy, Netherlands, Norway, Japan, South Korea, UK)
Novaya Zemlya
Labytnangi
Iqualuit
Kong Frederik VIII Land
SVALBARD (to Norway)
LONGYEARBYEN
Hornsund (Poland)
GREENLAND (to Denmark)
Summit Camp (USA)
Zackenberg
Greenland Sea
Limit of summer pack ice
Bjørnøya (to Norway)
Barents Sea
Kangerlussuaq
NUUK
Nuuk
Arctic Circle
Kong Christian IX Land
JAN MAYEN (to Norway)
Limit of winter pack ice
Norwegian Sea
Kevo
WSBS
Kilpisjarvi
Sodankyla
Sermilik
Denmark Strait
Alomar
Kiruna Observatory
Abisko
ICELAND
Myvatn
REYKJAVIK

0 km 250 500
0 miles 250 500

Climate – past and future

POLAR CLIMATES HAVE BEEN CHANGING ever since Earth was formed. Twenty million years ago, there was no ice at all in the polar regions. But, 20,000 years ago, Earth was in the grip of an ice age. Ice cores drilled from polar ice sheets show us records of these fluctuations on Earth and of changes in the atmosphere. We are now in a period of rapid warming, which seems to be caused by such changes. The effects of warming could be dramatic – on both the polar regions and the rest of the world.

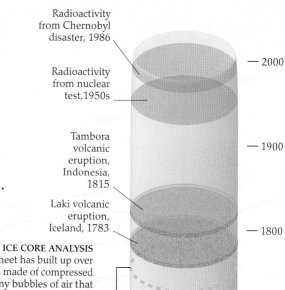

Radioactivity from Chernobyl disaster, 1986

Radioactivity from nuclear test, 1950s

Tambora volcanic eruption, Indonesia, 1815

Laki volcanic eruption, Iceland, 1783

ICE CORE ANALYSIS
The Greenland ice sheet has built up over thousands of years. It is made of compressed snow, which contains tiny bubbles of air that were trapped when it formed. These trapped bubbles can record air pollution and gases in the atmosphere, while the ice can record hanging temperatures. Scientists drill down into the ice and extract long ice cores for analysis. This diagram of a 1,000-year ice core from the Greenland ice sheet shows how it records events in the atmosphere over long time periods.

Little ice age – series of cold periods in northern hemisphere, 1450–1850

Orefajokull volcanic eruption, Iceland, 1362

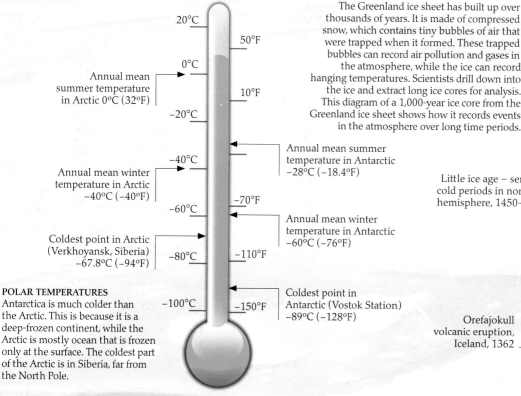

Annual mean summer temperature in Arctic 0°C (32°F)

Annual mean winter temperature in Arctic −40°C (−40°F)

Coldest point in Arctic (Verkhoyansk, Siberia) −67.8°C (−94°F)

Annual mean summer temperature in Antarctic −28°C (−18.4°F)

Annual mean winter temperature in Antarctic −60°C (−76°F)

Coldest point in Antarctic (Vostok Station) −89°C (−128°F)

POLAR TEMPERATURES
Antarctica is much colder than the Arctic. This is because it is a deep-frozen continent, while the Arctic is mostly ocean that is frozen only at the surface. The coldest part of the Arctic is in Siberia, far from the North Pole.

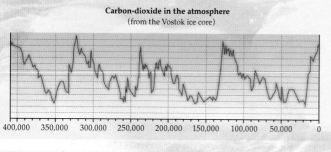

Carbon-dioxide in the atmosphere
(from the Vostok ice core)

400,000 · 350,000 · 300,000 · 250,000 · 200,000 · 150,000 · 100,000 · 50,000 · 0

CARBON DIOXIDE
The centre of the Antarctic ice sheet is known as the Vostok ice core. It has a record of changes in the atmosphere over at least 400,000 years. It shows that carbon dioxide (CO_2) levels have fluctuated since that time. Air samples since 1950 show much higher levels of this gas.

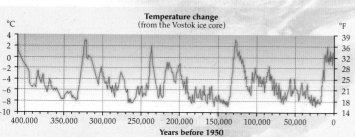

Temperature change
(from the Vostok ice core)

°C — 4, 2, 0, −2, −4, −6, −8, −10
°F — 39, 36, 32, 28, 25, 21, 18, 14

400,000 · 350,000 · 300,000 · 250,000 · 200,000 · 150,000 · 100,000 · 50,000 · 0

Years before 1950

TEMPERATURE
The ice in an ice core records changes in the local air temperature. The changes in temperature over the last 400,000 years match the fluctuations in carbon dioxide recorded in the same ice core. Since carbon dioxide in the air help to keep the planet warm, higher levels of this gas lead to higher temperatures.

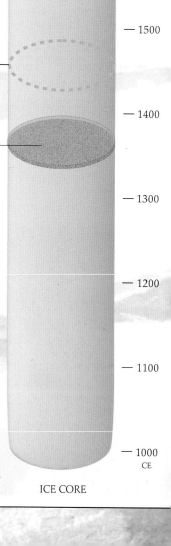

ICE CORE

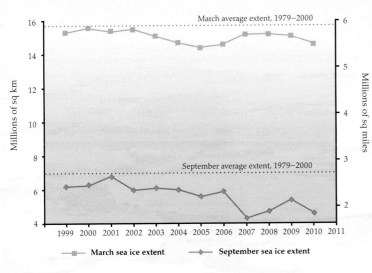

Larsen Ice Shelf in 1992, prior to the collapse in 1995

SEA ICE

Rising global temperatures are having a serious effect on the floating ice that forms on polar oceans. The Arctic sea ice is only half as thick as it was in 1960. Since 1979, the size of the frozen ocean in summer has shrunk by about 1.5 million sq km (600,000 sq miles) – an area twice the size of Texas, US. In winter, the ice sheet doubles in size. But the chart above shows that even the winter ice is shrinking. Each year is different, but the trend is down.

GREENHOUSE EFFECTS

• Earth's atmosphere acts as insulation that stops heat from escaping into space. Without it, the average global temperature would be 30°C (54°F) lower, the oceans would freeze, and life would be impossible. The insulation is called the greenhouse effect.

• The greenhouse effect is caused by certain gases in the atmosphere that absorb heat radiated by the planet. These "greenhouse gases" include carbon dioxide, methane, and nitrous oxide.

• If more carbon dioxide or other greenhouse gases are added to the atmosphere, they increase the greenhouse effect. As a result, the atmosphere retains more heat. This raises global temperatures.

• Air samples show that carbon dioxide levels in the air have been rising steadily since 1958. Climate records show that average global temperatures have been increasing at the same rate.

• It is likely that the rising temperatures are caused by the extra carbon dioxide in the air. This is released by burning coal, oil, and natural gas to fuel transport and generate electricity. The more fuel we burn, the more carbon dioxide is released, causing climate change.

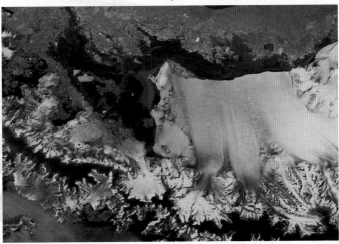

Larsen Ice Shelf in 1997, after the collapse in 1995

LARSEN ICE SHELF COMPARISON

The fringes of Antarctica are warming up faster than anywhere else on Earth. Average temperatures on the Antarctic Peninsula, near South America, have risen by up to 3°C (5.4°F) since 1951. The land here was once bordered by a floating ice shelf divided into three parts – Larsen A, B, and C. In 1995, Larsen A – on the left of this satellite image – broke up and the ice drifted away as icebergs, which eventually melted. In early 2002, the same happened to Larsen B, on the right. Ice shelves like these support the edges of the vast Antarctic ice sheets and their collapse could have serious consequences.

RISING SEA LEAVEL

This tiny island community is one of 280 inhabited coral islands in the Maldives, in the Indian Ocean. On average, the islands lie just 1.5 m (5 ft) above the waves. So any rise in sea level is a serious problem. The melting polar ice sheets are pouring vast amounts of meltwater into the warming oceans. The waves are already surging further inland at high tide. They swamp houses on some islands and contaminate freshwater supplies. Some scientists predict that global levels could rise by 88 cm (35 in) by the end of the century, which would be disastrous for the Maldives. But no one knows exactly when and how the polar ice sheets will melt. If they collapse suddenly, far more ice will slip into the sea, and coastal cities from New York, US to Shanghai, China could be under threat.

67

Species status

Polar animals are generally doing well compared with wildlife elsewhere, but they still face many challenges. Whale populations remain much reduced after past hunting. On oceanic islands, introduced rats and cats pose a threat to the seabirds that nest there. Many animals depend on sea ice for shelter or hunting. But global warming is melting sea ice, and there is some evidence that it will continue to do so. For marine mammals and birds, other problems include food shortages because humans catch their fish prey. They also face a risk of becoming entangled in fishing gear themselves.

EMPEROR PENGUIN

Scientific name: *Aptenodytes forsteri*

Location: Antarctica, breeding on sea ice attached to the mainland

Additional breeding colonies of emperor penguins have been discovered in recent years in Antarctica, boosting the known population of this still-thriving species. There are around 200,000 breeding pairs on Antarctic ice shelves.

ARCTIC FOX

Scientific name: *Alopex lagopus*

Location: Tundra regions all around the Arctic

The Arctic fox is protected in Scandinavia, where numbers are low. These versatile foxes are widespread in the rest of the Arctic and are not considered threatened overall.

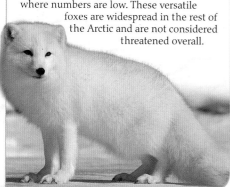

BLACK-BROWED ALBATROSS

Scientific name: *Thalassarche melanophrys*

Location: Breed on sub-Antarctic islands all around the Southern Ocean

There are an estimated 600,000 breeding pairs of this relatively common albatross. More than half breed on the Falkland Islands. However, their numbers are declining. They often get entangled in fishing gear and die.

WALRUS

Scientific name: *Odobenus rosmarus*

Location: Arctic Ocean, migrating to sub-Arctic areas in winter

Walrus on the Pacific Ocean side of the Arctic are larger and 10 times more numerous than those on the Atlantic side. To save them, each Inuit family is allowed to hunt only four a year.

POLAR BEAR

Scientific name: *Ursus marinus*

Location: Coasts and frozen seas of the Arctic and sub-Arctic

Decreasing amounts of Arctic sea ice, where polar bears do their hunting, is likely to drastically affect the future of this flagship species. Experts estimate the world's polar bear numbers at 20,000 to 25,000 at present.

BOWHEAD WHALE

Scientific name: *Balaena mysticetus*

Location: Arctic Ocean, migrating to sub-Arctic seas in winter

The bowhead is the only large whale to stay in northern waters all year round. This endangered animal was once heavily hunted and populations, especially on the Atlantic side of the Arctic, remain low.

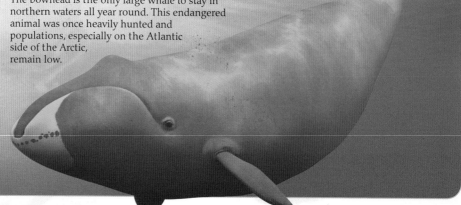

LEOPARD SEAL

Scientific name: *Hydrurga leptonyx*

Location: Antarctica and sub-Antarctic islands

This aggressive predator of other seals and penguins is not thought to be under threat at present. Estimates of its total population ranges to more than 400,000 individuals. Although it is known for its coat, it has escaped being hunted commercially for its skin.

ARCTIC WOLF

Scientific name: *Canis lupus arctos*

Location: Tundra of Canadian Arctic islands and Greenland

This whitish subspecies of the grey wolf lives in remote regions, where it hunts prey including the musk ox. Currently, it is not considered to be a threatened species.

SNOWY OWL

Scientific name: *Bubo scandiacus*

Location: Arctic tundra regions, sometimes flying south in winter

Found across northern North America and Eurasia, these versatile predators appear to be thriving. They hunt both by day and at night.

BELUGA WHALE

Scientific name: *Delphinapterus leucas*

Location: Arctic and north temperate waters, often among sea ice

Some southerly populations of this widespread species have declined, especially those in Canada's St Lawrence Estuary, whose health problems may be pollution-related.

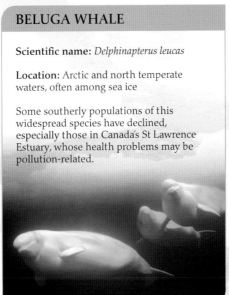

WOLVERINE

Scientific name: *Gulo gulo*

Location: North America and Eurasia, from Arctic to temperate regions

Wolverines were once trapped extensively for the fur trade. They now survive at low densities throughout many northern forests, mountain areas, and tundra lands.

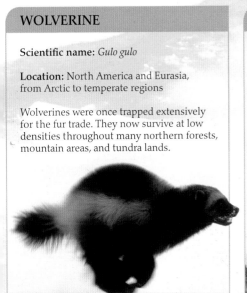

MUSK OX

Scientific name: *Ovibos moschatus*

Location: Tundra of northern Canada and Greenland (and reintroduced elsewhere)

Today, these hardy cousins of goats and sheep are flourishing and have been reintroduced to Alaska as well as to northern Eurasia where they last lived thousands of years ago.

Glossary

Siberian husky

ADAPTATION
A feature of a living thing that helps it thrive in its environment and lifestyle. Adaptations are passed on to offspring and evolve over generations.

ANTARCTIC CIRCLE
An imaginary line around the south polar region of Earth. South of the circle, there is at least one day of 24-hour daylight and one day of 24-hour darkness per year.

ANTARCTIC CONVERGENCE ZONE
A stormy zone in the oceans all around Antarctica, where cold sea water flowing from the Antarctic continent meets and sinks beneath warmer waters lying to the north.

ANTARCTIC PENINSULA
A point of land that stretches northwards towards South America on Antarctica's west side, with milder habitats than the rest of Antarctica.

ARCTIC CIRCLE
An imaginary line around the north polar region of Earth. North of the line, there is at least one day of 24-hour daylight and one day of 24-hour darkness per year.

AURORA
Also known as the Northern and Southern lights, flickering lights in the night sky sometimes visible in polar regions, caused by the interaction between high-energy particles from the Sun and the Earth's magnetic field.

Aurora australis (Southern Lights) at Amundsen–Scott South Pole Station

BERING SEA
A shallow, fertile sea lying south of the Bering Strait connecting the Arctic and the Pacific oceans.

BLUBBER
Fat that forms an insulating layer beneath the skin of whales, seals, and many seabirds.

Icebergs in Jokulsarlon glacier lagoon, Iceland

CARNIVORE
A meat-eating animal; in a narrower sense, a member of the order Carnivora, the mammal group that includes dogs, cats, bears, and seals.

CFCs
Short for chlorofluorocarbons, human-made industrial gases that have been shown to destroy the Earth's ozone layer.

COMB JELLY
Transparent jellyfish-like animals that swim in the plankton using rows of beating hair-like structures, called combs.

CORALS
Simple marine animals related to sea anemones. They grow in colonies fixed to a particular spot, supported by a skeleton, and grab their food from the passing water.

CRUSTACEANS
Invertebrate animals with jointed limbs and a hard outer skeleton.

FALKLAND ISLANDS
Islands in the South Atlantic lying due north of the Antarctic Peninsula, with milder climate.

GLACIER
A mass of land ice slowly flowing downhill.

GLOBAL WARMING
The current warming trend in Earth's atmosphere and oceans, thought to be due to increases in greenhouse gases.

GREENHOUSE GAS
Any gas in the atmosphere that tends to absorb heat radiating from the Earth's surface, causing the atmosphere to warm up.

HUSKY
A type of dog bred to pull sledge in Arctic areas.

ICE AGE
The alternating series of cold and milder spells that the Earth has experienced over the last 2.5 million years, and more specifically, the most recent cold spell ending around 10,000 years ago.

ICE CAP
A mass of permanent land ice similar to an ice sheet but smaller in extent.

ICE FLOE
A drifting section of broken-up sea ice.

ICE SHEET
A very large mass of permanent ice covering land.

ICE SHELF
An ice mass extending out to sea but attached to land and which begins as ice flowing from an ice sheet. It is 100–1,000 m (300–3,000 ft) thick,

INUIT
An ethnic group (or members of it) native to northernmost Canada and Greenland whose traditional lifestyle was intricately adapted to surviving in the Arctic environment.

INVERTEBRATE
Any animal without a backbone, including worms, snails, shrimps, starfish, and coral.

KRILL
Shrimp-like animals that swim and feed in huge numbers as part of the plankton of polar seas, and in turn are food for many larger animals.

LEAD
A channel of open water through sea ice.

LEMMINGS
Small, thick-furred mammals related to voles that are common inhabitants of the Arctic tundra and are important prey for larger animals.

LICHEN
Unique living organism that is an intimate partnership between a fungus and a simple plant (an alga). Small and hardy, lichens can grow as crusts on dry rocks or in leafy or bushy forms, such as the wrongly named reindeer moss.

MAMMAL
A warm-blooded animal, such as humans, dogs, cats, seals, deer, and whales, that suckles its young.

MIGRATION
A regular (usually yearly) large-scale movement of animals of a particular species from one region to another and back again. (A one-way journey, often caused by overcrowding or food shortage, is called an irruption.)

MOLLUSCS
A major group of invertebrate animals that includes snails, slugs, clams, octopuses, and squid, which share the same basic body plan despite their different shapes.

MOSS
Simple low-growing green plant that is non-flowering and lacks stems and roots.

NORTH POLE
The location at which Earth's axis (the imaginary line around which the Earth spins) reaches the surface of the Arctic Ocean.

OZONE LAYER
A region high in Earth's atmosphere containing the gas ozone (a form of oxygen) that protects life on Earth from harmful ultraviolet radiation.

PACK ICE
Drifting sea ice, especially when it has been broken up by wave action and then frozen together again.

PEAT
Dead plant material that has accumulated in cool, oxygen-free environments, such as bogs and fens, and as a result has not decayed.

PERMAFROST
Frozen ground found beneath the surface in polar regions. Ground frozen for two or more years continuously can be called permafrost, but some permafrost is thousands of years old.

PLANKTON
Plants or animals living in open water that cannot swim strongly and so drift with the currents. They are usually small or microscopic.

SCAVENGER
An animal that feeds on dead remains, usually of other animals or their food.

SCIENTIFIC NAME
The official name of a species, normally printed in *italic* type. It consists of two words, a genus name written with a capital letter, and a species name without one. For example, *Ursus maritimus* is the scientific name of the polar bear.

SEA ICE
Ice that has formed directly on the sea, in contrast to land-formed ice such as an ice shelf or iceberg. It is usually less than 5 m (15 ft) thick.

SEA URCHIN
Rounded, spiny, non-swimming sea animals related to starfish.

SHAMAN
A person in many traditional tribal societies who is regarded as having direct access to the spiritual world, and therefore is able to carry out functions such as curing illnesses and communicating with the dead.

SHELLFISH
A term for marine invertebrates that have hard outer shells, especially molluscs and crustaceans.

SOUTH POLE
The point at which Earth's axis (the imaginary line around which the Earth spins), reaches the surface of the Antarctic continent.

SQUID
Fast-swimming marine invertebrates of the open ocean related to octopuses, with two long tentacles and eight shorter arms.

Flock of snow geese in flight during migration

SUB-ANTARCTIC
Relating to regions north of Antarctica where conditions are less severe than in Antarctica itself. The phrase "sub-Antarctic islands" refers to any of the numerous islands dotting the ocean north of Antarctica.

SUB-ARCTIC
Relating to northern regions and habitats that are milder than the Arctic but colder than temperate lands. In marine terms, this includes seas of the north Pacific where there is some ice cover; on land, it refers to regions that have very cold winters but whose summers are warmer than those of the true Arctic.

SVALBARD
A group of Arctic islands north of, and belonging to, Norway. The main island is Spitsbergen.

TEMPERATE
Relating to the regions of the Earth with moderate temperatures between the tropics and the polar regions.

THERMAL
Relating to heat or temperature.

TRANSANTARCTIC MOUNTAINS
Longest mountain range in Antarctica, dividing the continent into East and West Antarctica.

TUNDRA
Treeless regions dominated by low-growing, cold-tolerant plants. Tundra is widespread in northern North America and Eurasia.

ULTRAVIOLET
Invisible high-energy light radiated from the Sun that can sometimes damage living things. Much of it is absorbed by the Earth's ozone layer.

Tundra landscape in Denali National Park, Alaska, USA

Index

Acknowledgements

Dorling Kindersley would like to thank:
Laurence Errington for the index; Monica Byles for proofreading; Open Air Cambridge Ltd. for the use of their clothing and equipment; the staff of Tierpark Dählhölzli, Bern, Switzerland, for their time and trouble; Tony Hall at the Royal Botanical Gardens, Kew; Julia Nicholson and the Pitt Rivers Museum, Oxford; Robert Headland and the staff of the Scott Polar Institute, Cambridge; Whipsnade Zoo, Bedfordshire; The British School of Falconry, Gleneagles, Scotland; Ivan Finnegan, Kati Poynor, Robin Hunter, Manisha Patel, Andrew Nash, Susan St. Louis, and Aude van Ryn for design and illustration assistance.
Additional photography: Lynton Gardiner at the American Museum of Natural History (60/61b); Neil Fletcher (1c); Dave King (37cr); Minden Pictures (42cl); Harry Taylor at the Natural History Museum (45tl, 47rt); University Museum, Cambridge (43cr); Jerry Young (16cl, 17c, 32/33, 40tl)
Maps: Sallie Alane Reason **Model:** Gordon Models

Picture credits
The publisher would like to thank the following for their kind permission to reproduce their photographs:

t=top b=bottom c=centre l=left r=right

Aardman Animations: 28cr Ardea: 36c; /Jean-Paul Ferrero 28bc; /François Gohier 45cr; /Graham Robertson 30c; B & C Alexander: 6/7b, 8bl, 11ctr, 15t, 21c, 23c, 25br, 38tl, 39tcr, 42bl, 42/43b, 44bl,

44br, 59c, 60cbl, 61cbr, 62tl, 62tr; /Paul Drummond 23tl; Barnaby's Picture Library /Rothman: 6/7c; Bridgeman Art Library: 25tl; / British Library 7tl; /National Maritime Museum 52cl; British Antarctic Survey: 10tr, 12ctl, 23bl; /D.G. Allan 13 tr, 13br; /C.J. Gilbert 10cl, 10bl, 12tl; /E. Jarvis 45br ; /B.; Thomas 61cr; Bruce Coleman Ltd: 14/15b, 34tl, 35bl, 36bl, 36br; Jen & Des Bartlett 20cl /Roger A. Goggan 12/13; /Johnny Johnson 7tr; /Stephen J. Krasemann 19br; /Len Rue Jr. 40bl; /Jon Shaw 41c; /Keith Nels Swenson 11ctl; /Rinie van Meurs 29cr; Corbis: Richard Baker / In Pictures 67bl; Michael S. Nolan / Terra 6-7b; Radius Images 69br; Denis Scott / Comet 68b; ET Archive: 6tr; Getty Images: Tom Brakefield / Photodisc 71tr; Yvette Cardozo / Workbook Stock 69c; Daniel J Cox / Photographer's Choice 69bl; Peter Lilja / The Image Bank 68c; Nathalie Michel / The Image Bank 69tl; Illustrated London News: 20tl, 26cr; Frank Lane Picture Agency: /Hannu Hautala 17tcl; /E&D Hosking 22c; /Peter Moore 14cl; /F. Pölking 32cl; /Mark Newman 38c; /Tony Wharton 17tl; Mary Evans Picture Library: 8tl, 9tr, 38tr, 40cr, 41tr, 42tl, 46tr, 54bl, 55ct, 55cr, 55bc, 56tl; NASA: 63tl; Goddard Space Flight Center Scientific Visualization Studio 67c; Courtesy of the National Science Foundation: Rhys Boulton 70cl; Natural History Photographic Agency: /B&C Alexander 10/11; /Melvin Grey 20/21b; /Brian Hawkes 29tl; /Tony Howard / ANT 10c; /E.A. James 29rr; /Peter Johnson 27c; /Stephen Krasemann 37tr; /Lady Philippa Scott 27bl; Robert Opie Collection: 59cr; Oxford Scientific Films: 27ctl; /Doug Allan 12c, 12b, 16bl, 30tl, 44ctr; /Michael Brooke 22tl; /S.R. Maglione 14/15t; /Colin Monteath 22b; /S.R. Morris 35cl; /Owen

Newman 20ctl; /Ben Osborne 26bl, 28l, 29b; /Richard Packwood 36tl; /Konrad Wothe 32bcr; Planet Earth Pictures: /Gary Bell 33tcl; /Peter Scoones 29tc; /Scott McKinley 9cr; /Bora Merdsoy 13bl; Royal Geographical Society: 53cr, 53tr, 56cl; /Alastair Laidlaw 53br; Science Photo Library: /Dr. David Millar 63bl; /Claude Nuridsany & Marie Perennou 62cl; Zefa Picture Library: /Allstock 31c; /Frans Lanting 26tl

Jacket images: Front: Dorling Kindersley: Jerry Young; Science Photo Library: Simon Fraser c; Back: Dorling Kindersley: Scott Polar Research Institute, Cambridge cb, University Museum of Zoology, Cambridge cr, Jerry Young ca

Wallchart: Bryan & Cherry Alexander / ArcticPhoto: cl/ (walrus); Dorling Kindersley: The American Museum of Natural History cr, Gordon Models - modelmaker ftl, Natural History Museum, London fcra; Getty Images: Arctic-Images / Iconica fbl/ (tern), Stone / Kevin Schafer bc; Photolibrary: Oxford Scientific (OSF) / Doug Allan fbl, cra, Peter Arnold Images / Jonathan Bird tr; Photoshot: NHPA / Bryan and Cherry Alexander Photography fcla
All other images © Dorling Kindersley
For further information see: www.dkimages.com

Every effort has been made to trace the copyright holders. Dorling Kindersley apologises for any unintentional omissions and would be pleased, in such cases, to add an acknowledgement in future editions.